Open the Coffin

Open the Coffin

✦

A true story of the supernatural

Paul Casey

iUniverse, Inc.

New York Lincoln Shanghai

Open the Coffin
A true story of the supernatural

Copyright © 2005 by Paul Casey

iUniverse books may be ordered through booksellers or by contacting:

iUniverse
2021 Pine Lake Road, Suite 100
Lincoln, NE 68512
www.iuniverse.com
1-800-Authors (1-800-288-4677)

ISBN-13: 978-0-595-35654-6 (pbk)
ISBN-13: 978-0-595-67255-4 (cloth)
ISBN-13: 978-0-595-80132-9 (ebk)
ISBN-10: 0-595-35654-0 (pbk)
ISBN-10: 0-595-67255-8 (cloth)
ISBN-10: 0-595-80132-3 (ebk)

Printed in the United States of America

CONTENTS

PREFACE

Only an eyelid away lies another world.

Dreams, ghosts, psychic events, numerology, cards, astrology, all are discovering an unlikely ally in the advancing wave of theoretical science. It is the voice of the universe itself.

Regarding themes such as the story of this book, perhaps the most revealing background of its author lies in more typical samples of his work. The following essay was written in response to an invitation from the International Biographical Center in Cambridge, England, on the future of traditional science in the Twenty-First Century.

◆　　◆　　◆

NEW CENTURY PHYSICS—A RETURN
TO THE PROPHETS?
essay in 900 words

The answers to fundamental questions are not in the details of how things happen, but in the summation, the consequences of behavior.

SUPPOSE YOU WERE TOLD:

    a. The universe does not contain everything that exists.

    b. It was called into being for a reason. It has a task and a purpose. It is a time/space tool.

c. Gravity is not a force of attraction between bodies; it is the reduction of space, inversely with the expansion of its co-function, time.

d. Black holes are not the sites of tremendous gravitational forces. They are the opposite, the condition where all forces are disappearing.

e. The universe will neither continue expanding nor collapse back upon itself; it will simply shut down. It is happening already.

f. The end product of the universe is equilibrium, the preexisting nonphysical state that triggered its prescribed operation in the beginning.

Physics, as it is practiced today, is scientific superstition. Born of the same human intrigues that drove the old explorers, modern astrophysicists are today tantalized by the volume of new data made available with the Spitzer telescope, producing more and more detail about what things are and how they work. But what is the Achilles' heel in this picture?

Science believes itself because the math seems to work. It is the old I.Q. test again. It seemed to work, but it didn't measure what we thought we were measuring. Like the magician's vanishing act, the illusion only works over a limited angle of vision. What is being missed is the fundamental question of why all this marvel exists in the first place.

What is the most obvious phenomenon we see when we look out across the galaxy, across the universe? Forces at work. But forces only occur where things are out of balance. We learned that as children, when the big guy got off the other end of the teeter-totter. What does this tell us? The universe is in a condition of imbalance. We even encode its behavior into the so-called Laws of Conservation, that "everything tends toward equilibrium." In other words, everything the universe is doing prescribes its ultimate goal to be equilibrium. Therein lies the challenge for future physics. It is the angle of vision beyond the magician's trick.

With equilibrium comes the cessation of all action, even within the tiniest of subnuclear particles. In the absence of action, the measuring sticks of time and space no longer apply. Mass itself loses all identity. We know this. It should mean something to us besides its standard acceptance. It should ring a very loud bell.

Our new generations raised on cyber-space games will have no trouble getting the implication. The universe engages our physical senses, even our interaction, but like the cyber-space games, it only contains the information it is programmed to conclude. In operation, it is not unlike a computer maintenance program, "Defrag" or "Norton Utilities," evoked to stabilize the integrity of a more fundamental order.

And what is that order? Traditional physics has always had it upside down.

Principles of order and consequences are the prerequisite even for a simple chemical reaction, yet they are not part of the mass/energy performance. They represent a superior state of discipline, which is not dependent upon temporary phenomena. The universe had a beginning and will have an end, which automatically places it in the slave position. A reconciliation of these priorities is important for our theoretical frontiers to move forward.

An essential part of any self-governing system is its stabilizing safeguards. The reason the universe looks as if it was created in a Big Bang, is that it arrived as a full-blown program, booted-up to preserve the stability of the equilibrium. It is a necessary feature of the primordial (nonmaterial) system.

Envisioning the universe as a time/space tool, gravity now becomes the dynamic balancing of these two components. Simply, as time expands, space is reduced correspondingly. What we mistakenly perceive as a law of attraction between bodies is actually the disappearance of space between the bodies. One might say that particles eat space. It looks the same and acts the same, but the implications are vastly different. It means that gravity is not a force in the sense that we now regard it. It is further observed in the apparent time/space warp that Einstein believed he detected around large bodies like the earth. We should expect it. The difference is that the internal space of a large mass has already been vastly reduced in comparison to the open space around it. The amount of space being consumed is the same, but consumed in a different pattern.

A computer displays the processing of data only as long as it is performing the task. Traditional physics describes black holes as sites of tremendous gravitational forces sucking everything around them into virtual oblivion. But set aside our presumptions for a moment and contemplate what we are actually observing. The fact that all mass appears to become compressed and even light unable to escape does not mean that tremendous forces are acting upon them. How can we say this? Because if the forces are disappearing that allow us to see them, it would appear exactly the same to human technology. Black holes are sites of conversion to zero mass, where the process is ending. Nothing is going anywhere. Regions of data are simply being restored to their native nonmaterial address and out of our optical range.

In the body language of its own behavior, the goal of the universe is to put itself out of business. But no law says that it has to happen everywhere all at once. It is already full of holes. As a maintenance program, it will neither expand forever nor collapse back upon itself. Where each task is completed, it will shut down. We see it happening already.

In short, advanced physics of this new century will look startlingly like the visions of the ancient prophets. The difficulty for our next generation of physicists will be to re-train our parameters. By its own hard evidence, science must inevitably shift its definitions of existence into the terms of equilibrium, in other words, the realm of spirit.

from Universal Mechanics
© 7-15-02 by Paul Casey

◆   ◆   ◆

Why was this book not written thirty years ago, when it happened? It is something one usually holds private among friends, especially if he is known professionally as a scientist. Moreover, its events are still ongoing to this day. But the world has changed. Never before has there been such need for concrete evidence that life does indeed continue beyond the grave. It is time the story be told.

OPEN THE COFFIN is a double metaphor, not only for life outside the box of time and space, but also the exposure of a crime and cover-up that has lain buried for these past five centuries.

Far beyond those six days of seemingly impossible happenings, May of 1974 was the first show of bone to a great skeleton of bizarre connections, past, present and future.

Suddenly dredging up into consciousness, it could only picture the creature of a long-term affair.

Let the pundits have their field day. We just say, "What do you do with the evidence?" We were there.

The DREAM   The AUTHOR

A TALE FROM THE TOMB

The PSYCHIC   The CAT

February, 1971

Africa

with
Meredith

Photos by Paul Casey

Cathedral of Burgos, where Philip's Requiem Mass was held

The ancient town of Tordesillas, *Spain*
where Juana was imprisoned for years in a room without light

MAXIMILIAN'S TRIUMPHAL ARCH
Central panel

Detail

Queen Juana I of Spain

Philip *the handsome* of Austria

Woodcuts by Albricht Dürer 1512

Los Angeles Times

LARGEST CIRCULATION IN THE WEST

FIVE PARTS—PART ONE

MONDAY MORNING, MARCH 29, 1965

90 PAGES

KILLER QUAKE

ar Hundreds Dead in Ch

FINAL
Draft and
Our Youth
—March of Events

Entire Village Buried as Massive Temblor Breaks 230-Foot Dam

SANTIAGO (AP) — A massive earthquake shook and shattered a 1,200-mile-long strip of Chile at noon Sunday, burying a village of 400 people, killing at least 23 others and leaving thousands homeless and injured.

The village of El Cobre disappeared when a 230-foot-high dam burst, dumping two million tons of water on the copper m...
Santiago. The village is m...
30-foot deluge from...
used in operation at...
Cobre Company...
Other deaths and injuries we...

Sunday, Mar. 29, 1964   CCCS Los Angeles Herald-Examiner   A-3

Death Temblor Looses Wave of Destruction

HERALD EXAMINER
LOS ANGELES EVENING AND SUNDAY

Associated Press
London Daily Express
Hearst Headline Service
United Press International • N.Y. Times News Service
Dow Jones
CLASSIFIED ADVERTISING Richmond 8-1211

SUNDAY, MARCH 29, 1964

Alaskans Buried by Earthqu
California Tidal Wave Kills 1

SASTER!

L.A. Plane Lost at Sea, 305

(Story i

SUNNY

The

EARTHQUAKE DREAMS

a year of preparation

The
BIRTH CARD
Connection

2 ♥   **9 ♠**

Venus

8 of Clubs
December 10

"When the psychic
power is extreme
(as in some cases),
unless great care is
taken for protection,
they become fields for
possible invasion."...

♂

Mars

Jack
♠

8 of Clubs card

Ace of Diamonds
November 6

"In general, this is a card
of sorrow, usually hidden.
... secrecy in connection
with associations, either
business or personal.
Her natural ambitions are
too likely to meet with
insurmountable obstacles.
Emotions play a large part
and it becomes a race
between love and money."

♃

Jupiter

Ace of Diamonds card

A ♥

Saturn

*Sacred Symbols
of the
Ancients*
Randall & Campbell

5 ♦   **7 ♣**

an extract from the
MUNDANE SPREAD

Tracy

Myself

John

Meredith

Norman

Udana

Katangi

Jeryll & Frodo

WE WERE THERE.

- with Anna Bing Arnold

Carole Lombard's old house

THE
PLAY

Los Angeles Playwrights Group

Franklin & Glady Lacey

with Van Johnson

with Beatrice Lillie

The California
SPANGLED
CATS

Neiman
Marcus

His & Hers
Gift of the Year

Christmas Book
of 1986

CALIFORNIA
SPANGLED CAT

SIDE-TRACKED

Madison Square
Garden

"Mona Lisa"

filmed a scene
with
Mel Gibson
for
Lethal Weapon

Canned-hunt killers   Court House, Belize City

A
JUNGLE
CRUSADE

Lamanai
archaeological site

SOLENZ™

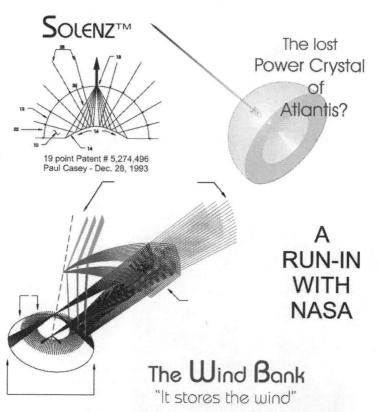

19 point Patent # 5,274,496
Paul Casey - Dec. 28, 1993

The lost
Power Crystal
of
Atlantis?

A
RUN-IN
WITH
NASA

The Wind Bank
"It stores the wind"

Patents pending

A reading at the
STELLA ADLER MAIN THEATRE
Hollywood

James Morrison

Riad Galayini

Susan Clark

'Juana'!
The story is extraordinary.
Vividly written and passionate.

Ken B

KENNETH BRANAGH

1

All our lives we struggle with a world in linear time. Yet the moment we fall asleep, a most extraordinary thing happens. We slip outside the box. We all do it.

Thin halos of mist clung to the street lights as I returned from my run across UCLA campus and ascended the old iron stairs at the back of the building on Weyburn Avenue. It was more like a fire-escape than a staircase, and my footsteps gave low ringing sounds that bounced off the walls across the empty parking lot behind me. At half-past eleven, the building was now deserted, and only the little 60 watt bathroom lights were on at the top.

Inside I could hear Katangi the cat greet my arrival from my office down the hall, but I stopped to wash up, before heading back to the typewriter.

The night still rattled of Watergate, the energy crisis, Vietnam, the Middle East, Northern Ireland—things to blot out, as I headed into my deadline on the teleplay. Its brilliant final scenes, so meticulously worked out during my run, existed only in ephemeral memory and would use any excuse to collapse before I could get it all down on paper. It promised to be a long night ahead.

But I was barely back at my desk a few minutes, when an extreme drowsiness dropped over me like a net. It was so unexpected and intense I remember thinking at the time,

"How can this possibly be, when I'm so pumped-up from running?"

For maybe a dozen more sentences, I tried to work on through it, but soon my eyes just froze on a few words and wouldn't go any further. The veins in my arms and legs seemed to be pooling with the force of gravity. But by now I knew what it was, and I allowed it to continue. I had had such episodes before. Something primal in my subconscious was moving.

With the dizziness that accompanies it, I locked up the office and made my way down the hall to my little store room at the rear of the building, keeping a hand against the wall. There I had a small fold-out bed. But by this time I was so ready to close my eyes I just laid down on a pad on the floor and slipped into a deep sleep immediately.

Presently and without any apparent transition, the sun was high above and to my left. I found myself about thirty feet off the ground, descending toward the outer bounds of some European castle. It was grey in color. The stretch of land behind me was green, probably early summer, and in the distance stood a number of plume-shaped trees bordering some kind of waterway. I came to rest on a retaining wall, which supported the earthen works that sloped up to the main structure.

For a moment I turned and looked around. I had never seen the place before. There stood a young man about six feet tall, with shoulder length blond hair, wearing a fancy cap, elegant blue tunic, fitted trousers and tan boots. He looked about twenty and did not acknowledge my presence, but continued giving orders to three workmen in a language that sounded like German. On the flats below, the other men were in brown and moving timbers for some reason. I couldn't understand them, which was puzzling at the time, since I had taken three semesters of German in college.

It seemed later that I might have been facing east. But anyway, directly ahead of me, a wing of the castle extended out flush with the wall.

Like a Time-Cut, I was suddenly standing in one of its upper suites, my attention centered upon a most lovely young woman, who was seated on a lounge toward the middle of the room. The information just popped into my head. It never occurred to me to wonder how. "My God," I told myself, "It's Juana!"

"And the man down on the wall must be Philip," I deduced. "No wonder I couldn't understand him. He's speaking old Austrian."

She was Juana of Trastamara, the middle child of Isabella and Fernando, the fearsome monarchs of Spain. Also looking about nineteen or twenty, she sat alone in the room, her rich auburn hair pulled back under a coverlet. Her eyes were medium brown, her mouth smallish and pretty. And although she was facing my direction, she did not look directly at me. She just seemed to be thinking.

The rest of the room was less clear, mainly an impression of red draperies, a vaulted ceiling, no windows on the opposite wall behind her, but a great tapestry with furniture beneath it. A large figured rug covered the middle of the floor. There were doors to my right, but I never looked at them. I could think of nothing but the ghastly stories, the grisly legends of what was to befall her, and my heart spasmed with pain.

"Oh, my god, what can I do to help her?" was all I could think. "—The horrendous life she's going to have!"

Now, even worse, I detected that she was several months pregnant, carrying the very child who will imprison her for years in a room without light,—rob and torment her. She will die a mad woman. It was almost too monstrous to contemplate.

"What can I tell her?" I anguished over and over, "She'll never believe it! She'll never believe that all the heirs to the throne ahead of her are going to die. Four of them. She'll be Queen of half the world. She'll never believe it—!"

How could she, this vibrant girl, her whole life ahead of her, daughter of kings, with an impassioned young husband—? How could she even imagine that all the men she loves will betray her,—that before ten years are out, she will wander the land with a rotting corpse and die in prison with the burns of scalding water...? Oh, my god, it was so awful, I could not bear it.

"Oh, Juana..!" my cries seemed captive inside my skull. Finally I blurted out, "Don't trust the people who are surrounding you. They are making you a prisoner!"

She flinched. BANG! Perhaps from my own outcry I was hyper-awake, every hair standing on end. It was so vivid, I knew I was really there.

May 14th, 1974.

2

*As I say, our perception of linear time is not
always the way things happen. And to
understand why I knew about Juana to begin
with, one needs to go back four years.*

November, 1970. I was surprised by a phone call from North
Dakota. The daughter of an eminent horse veterinarian from
the border of Montana, Meredith had been recently widowed
by the death of my dad's cousin Clement.

She was a familiar face to animal rights crusaders across
the country, even producing a weekly television show. The
flashy Sophia Loren type had more than once camped on the
White House steps to vocalize her messages against the big
farmers' machine-gunning of wild horses from the air, and
the crating of little mustangs to be broken in the rodeos of
Texas, on their way to the slaughter house.

It was great to hear from her.

"My gosh," I brightened, "What a surprise. Are you in town?"

"No, no, I'm back at the ranch," she had told me, "But I hear
you're going to Spain."

"..Oh, right—!" I laughed, "You just caught me."

("I hear you're going to Spain—" ??) At the time I had taken
it as a joke. I wasn't planning anything at all.

"Any chance you could put up with a companion?" she went
on.

"What do you mean?" I sobered.

"Well, I finally settled the estate, and I just need to get away for a while," she said, "We've always been sympatico. So, I thought if you wouldn't mind throwing in Africa and London and Rome, if you've got the time, I've got the money."

She was serious.

Needless to say, it didn't take any arm-twisting. Meredith sent the money and left the details to me. Our tentative dates were set for February and March.

The point is, why had she said that? "I hear you're going to Spain?" I had never asked her.

For three decades Generalissimo Francisco Franco had run an iron-fisted military dictatorship, hardly a big tourist attraction. Neither of us spoke Spanish, and truth be known, I actually didn't consider it in our original itinerary. Yet, by a circuitous chain of events, we ended up going there anyway.

That year, period pieces were hot, with the opening of Glenda Jackson's "Elizabeth," and the trip offered a rare opportunity to research some other worthwhile figure in history. But who? All the obvious ones were done to death.

All through November and December I had haunted the libraries, foraging for something fresh. But it seemed a field ploughed-over too many times. I was about to abandon the hope, when one late afternoon, riding back to the office with Norman my agent, he stopped to deliver something to Bob Chapman, another client and amateur historian.

"I just put down the most fascinating book," was Bob's greeting to us at the door. It was Townsend-Miller's *The Castles and the Crown,* with a short chapter on Juana la loca, the queen who went mad over the death of her husband.

"You know, some old cryptic letters recently turned up in the archives of the Spanish Treasury," Bob went on to tell, "between her keepers in Tordesillas and the foreigners on her throne."

The mysterious letters he was referring to had disappeared for four and a half centuries and made reference to the extreme risk of allowing anyone to see the imprisoned queen.

In those days it was the belief that the only cure for insanity was quiet isolation, and for years she was kept in a windowless room, having no contact at all with the outside world. Could their fear have been that visitors would worsen her condition? Or was it something more sinister? If she was not insane, the peril of that discovery would certainly require the extreme secrecy in which she was held by the Austrian surrogates and puppet Prince who ruled in her place.

For a total of thirty years the only word that seeped out of her prison was gossip. It was that intrigue and the chance encounter with Bob that really put Spain on the itinerary.

Almost five decades of Juana's isolation and four intervening centuries had left little of her real story intact. Half-truths, contradictory reports and morbid legends had scattered it about in a puzzle of arcane documents, ship's logs, church records and little snippets in biographies of her contemporaries.

With so little to go on, we also spent weeks searching for a mysterious book purported to be about Juana. We knew it existed and was written in English. But no one remembered the title, the author or publisher. Bottom line, we could never find it.

—Came February and a tale of "unbelievable luck."

I touched down in New York at the height of a white-out blizzard, twenty minutes late and the last flight to get in. Delayed passengers were camped everywhere, and it was a slalom to the other terminal, where Meredith was waiting. As I spied her, I was also relieved to see that our connecting flight was still on the ground.

Canny Meredith, as usual, had anticipated the bad weather and arrived a day early. Even from a distance she was easy to spot among the throng at the gate,—a beacon in lavender mink.

"I didn't think you'd make it," she widened her eyes, as we met in a hug. "Would you believe this? Everything's been grounded for hours."

"Yeah," I panted, "They were going to divert us to Dulles, right up to the last minute."

Surveying the mink, I chided, "Fur? Meredith—!"

"I know. I hate it," she said. "I'll throw it away as soon as we get back."

"May I have your attention please?," a voice interrupted on the loud speakers, "They tell us that a little window is opening up here, so please stand by to board, in case this flight is able to depart. If you will form a line at the gate, please have your tickets ready and carry-on luggage in hand."

"That's us!" Meredith said.

That quick, like an omen, our flight was off and away, the last flight out, as the blizzard shut down New York again for the rest of the day.

It set the tone for the entire trip, as if it were charmed. Nairobi was ablaze with brilliant colored flags and spectacular costumes from all over the continent—the great Pan African Trade Fair of 1971—the one and only time that all nations of Africa would ever gather together in a single event.

At tent camp on the Mara River, just for the two of us, we were surprised to find unscheduled visitors. Africa's leading ornithologist, Tony Dean and his wife had arrived at the same place, at the same time to photograph birds for his new book. And for the next three days, they hosted us on game drives with a depth of knowledge that only a native scientist could possibly provide.

Lobo Lodge, perched high atop an outcropping of giant boulders on the Serengeti, came exactly upon the full moon. There we sat, Meredith and I, eating strawberries and ice cream at midnight on the terrace, while below a million year old scene played out in the silence—herds of elephants, wildebeests, antelope and zebra drifting past along the great migration corridor.

A year before, publicist Rupert Alan had arranged a dinner for me with Dr. Louis S. B. Leakey in Beverly Hills, so Meredith and I continued on into Tanzania to his famous archaeological digs at Olduvai Gorge. There, at a little monument to "Zinjanthropus," we stood upon the site of ancient man. It was as if our very souls were being stretched to a timeless state, in preparation for what was to come.

While the weather remained perfect the entire time, only the oldest of the game wardens at Amboseli had ever witnessed a congregation of animals in such numbers as they did that season. And returning to Nairobi, we were perhaps the only non-Africans who hadn't lost their accommodations to the massive influx of native participants in the fair.

By the last afternoon, as we were invited for tea in the owners' boxes at the horse races, we had become all too aware of our unlikely run good fortune. The famous "Luck o' the Irish" could only account for it. Then, of course, came Spain.

"Things still happen in Spain that the outside world knows nothing about," Rupert had said before we left. As publicist for the principality of Monaco, Princess Grace, the National Geographic, Steve McQueen, Liza Minelli, Jacqueline Bisset, and whomever, he was a highly credible person not given to exaggeration. And he had related a tale told him by one of his clients. The man had sworn it was absolutely true. He and his bride had been on their honeymoon.

In Burgos they had done something that was intended to be romantic. They had hidden out one night in the old cathedral, until everyone left and it was all locked up. They wanted to experience the moonlight shining in through the great stained-glass windows. Which they did. Then they crawled into a niche and went to sleep, planning to make their exit as soon as the people began coming in again in the morning.

However, they were wakened some time later by low chanting and a procession of black-hooded monks, bringing with them a young girl all in white. She looked as if she were in a trance. Of course, the couple was afraid to be caught, so they remained hidden, while the procession passed on by and out of sight.

But before long, the mass ended. They heard the girl let out a cry of alarm, then there was the scraping sound of heavy stone-on-stone, and the girl's muffled cries went silent. When the monks passed by again on their way out, the girl was no longer with them.

Horrified, their hair standing on end, the couple immediately went scurrying to see if they could find out what happened to the girl. But there was no sign of anyone—or anything—just dozens and dozens of silent old crypts. They were certain that they had witnessed a black mass and that the girl lay somewhere under one of those huge marble slabs, on top of whatever was already in there.

The old cathedral at Burgos guards the remains of El Cid himself and was also the place where Requiem Mass had been held for Philip. Our first sight of it drew tingles.

Huge, dark and ominous, it rises from the base of the hill to dominate the whole city, with its needle-spires stretching the vaulted towers on upward toward heaven, like prayers turned to stone. We knew that its impervious walls concealed hidden chambers and courtyards, where cloistered and countless human beings live out their lives, unknown even to those on the streets a few feet away.

In the awesome cavity of its basilica, one feels exposed and vulnerable. As we passed its aisles and naves, we could not help but wonder if beneath those exquisite marble effigies of ancient knights and nobles there might lie...others.

In stark contrast, our next morning took us again to the open spaces. It was the farming district to the south, its fields stretching out in every direction, clean and fragrant with dry grass under the warming sun. Before we even rolled to a stop at the roadside, we could see the crumbling little castle on the hill, just as described in the books. We had arrived at Hornillios.

Over the centuries, the fateful journey that had brought Juana to this place had swollen into legend, the so-called mortuary cult. But what could the ignorant peasants have known, anyway? They simply woke in the night to the eerie specter of chanting monks passing in the fog with flapping robes and torches, a great royal coffin and a woman all in black.

"She wanders all over Spain with the rotting corpse," they whispered, "—gone mad for the loss of her Prince. She believes that her love will bring him back to life."

We got out to look around. The only evidence of a real settlement was a cluster of old farmhouses set back off the road and grouped around a tiny dirt plaza. If accounts can be believed, at least a few of the dwellings dated back far enough that Juana surely would have seen them with her own eyes. It invoked a sort of magical feeling. No one knows whether the actual building still exists where the queen of an empire gave birth to her posthumous child, while its father lay waiting the infant's cry in a coffin out under the trees.

We seemed to be alone, when from nowhere, who should pop up but the mayor himself. A robust and grinning middle-aged farmer arrived with two buddies, who couldn't take their eyes off of Meredith. "She is the Queen of America," they agreed.

We were aware that mayor has a different connotation in Spanish, but our own version was more fun to tell. Pointing to the crumbling ruins on the hill, he proudly announced that it was none other than the castillo de Juana-loca. The truth didn't matter. The spell of romance was more telling than the facts, and an invitation to take wine at his table was eagerly accepted.

Its doorknobs hammered by blacksmith and walkways decorated by hand, the old farmhouse had changed little for generations, thanks in part to Franco's oppressive regime and isolation since the end of World War II. It was yet another slip-zone into the past. There, among the timeless people of the countryside, we sipped wine from the vines in the yard and aged in those curious shallow holes along the path to the ruins on the hill.

But it was the dark attic at the top of a ladder, where I sensed the real ghosts and secrets. Strings of tallow drippings and garlic hung from the wooden beams, lending their essence to the bundles of woolen blankets and sacks of grain that slumped in the corners. Centuries of it were trapped in the wood all around, as I sat for minutes with my eyes closed, just drawing it in. I wasn't alone. Doing much the same, a rat-cat sat on guard in the window.

I could look down into a goat pen outside the kitchen, where three newborn kids cuddled in a box of hay and bright feathered chickens strutted about on their serious quest for anything peckable.

Outside beneath the trees, I came upon evidence of another old building that had once stood there. But no one living could say whether it had been a house or a barn. It had long fallen to fungus and weather before any of them were born.

In a last round of handshakes, we headed off to rendezvous with what was to be the most extraordinary event of the entire trip.

Upon the bridge of many arches spanning the brown Duero River, we approached at last the ancient town of Tordesillas. Perhaps because of its notorious reputation and terrible things that had happened there, the grim old castle of curses and ghosts was long torn down, which had been the place of Juana's imprisonment and death in 1555.

Even beyond that, it was bizarre, a spooky sensation. The whole town was deserted, not a single soul in sight, except for one solitary man in a business suit standing by his car in plain view.

"Must be siesta," I muttered.

"Or an ambush," Meredith added.

Watching us arrive, the man almost appeared to be waiting for us. Since there was obviously no one else, we drove up to ask him directions.

"I know it's torn down, now, but there used to be an old castle here," I said, "Do you happen to know where it was?"

He didn't speak English, and I didn't speak Spanish, but we both knew German well enough to converse. Smiling amusedly, he answered, "We meet on the castle."

Its foundations were right beneath us.

"I'm looking for information about Juana la loca," I told him.

"Ah, then you have a special good luck," he grinned again. "I live in Madrid and only come this way on business a couple of times a year to stop for gas and lunch, but I happen to have the keys to the vault where her last possessions are kept. Come on, I'll show you."

Weirded-out, Meredith and I exchanged a glance and followed him. What had begun as a lighthearted and charmed trip had turned truly eerie. Of the two weeks we spent in Spain, five minutes earlier or five minutes later, we would have missed him.

We followed in silence across the street and into a building, where he unlocked the old iron door of a cramped stone vault. There, the last things that Juana had touched were waiting—her lovely guitar, combs, candlesticks—waiting for us. It really felt that way.

Of course, all that said,—all that behind us, when I returned to Westwood, period pieces were out, and Norman had lined me up with a number of meetings.

I put all my notes into a drawer of the old Fortress file cabinet, where they sat undisturbed for the next three years.

3

The full impact of the dream was rooted in yet earlier events of 1964, a year of preparation and my first acquaintance with the connotations of number eleven.

I had spent the year in Alaska, photographing wildlife and eventually taking over the produce department of a grocery store in Anchorage. It belonged to Aunt Carmen and Uncle Danny, and my bedroom was on the second floor over the market.

One night I was wakened by the sound of a masculine voice clearly and loudly saying, "Get out."

"Hm. Yes," I thought, "It's time I get back to California." I picked up the phone, made the reservations and went back to sleep. It happened so quickly, only Aunt Hazel knew I was returning. She picked me up at LAX.

Within a few days, I began working for Magical Productions, a machine shop on Venice Boulevard, which built illusions and props for Mark Wilson's Magic Castle television show for children, as well as robotics for Vegas acts and trade shows.

It's a separate world of its own,—where competitive magicians wandered in off the street in disguise to spy on us,—where Bob Fenton, our own shell-shocked eccentric, speed-read three to four paperbacks a day,—where the Great Grimaldi slept in a parachute in a warehouse full of things that didn't work, and the business at hand was levitating six women at a time. The salient point is, the icy Cook Inlet and pristine Chugach Mountains of Alaska were about as far as they could possibly be from my mind.

One Wednesday morning, about 4:30 A.M. and still dark, I wakened from the most elaborate dream. I had been back in California such a brief time that I was still sleeping on Hazel's couch and looking for a place to rent.

"Some shrink would love to get hold of me," I told Hazel, recounting it later at breakfast.

"I dreamed I was back in Anchorage, when this enormous earthquake began. Huge cracks opened up in the ground, parked cars were bashing into each other, buildings slid off their foundations," I could feel the shaking as if I were actually there. "The whole middle of town was like sinking into the ground. I was helping people get everything out of their houses,—bird cages, everything. At one point I saw Danny almost fall into one of those fissures, and he barely got out before it closed up again."

Hazel and I mused over the amazing detail of it, until I headed off to work.

Later the same day, I recounted the dream to Virginia Lynne, who was writing radio shows at the time for the Salvation Army. And that night, I mentioned it again to Tracy Morgan, a longtime friend.

A statuesque ex-Miss California with a mane of red hair and famous bosoms, Tracy was one of the last MGM starlets, along with Dyan Cannon. Half Irish and half gypsy, she was also a well known psychic, who occasionally worked with the police department and even did readings for Peter Hurkos himself.

Thursday. Thursday, I just put it out of my mind.

But Friday, I was only at work half an hour, when a dizzying nausea overwhelmed me, with a hard pulsing in my neck and forehead. It was as one might feel to have someone you love crushed under a steamroller right before your eyes.

The worst of it passed, but the nausea persisted, and I was prompted to call and see if everyone in the family was all right. I first called Hazel, because she was the oldest and the nearest. I didn't tell her why.—She was fine.

Then I called Mom. She was okay. I called my brothers. They were okay. I made a couple more calls. Then I thought, well, sure I'm going crazy. Still, I couldn't shake the sick feeling.

I finally told Johnny Gaughn, the shop foreman, "I'm too sick. I can't stay. I've got to go home."

Anyway, by the time I got back to Hazel's I felt fine and I just did some work around the house. Then around 6:00 or 6:30 in the evening, the calls started. "My God, have you heard about the earthquake in Anchorage?—Over eight points. All the power is knocked out. The phones are down. No one knows anything."

Hazel and I sat looking at each other—in between the calls. "Carmie and Danny are okay," I told her, "I saw them in the dream. I need to tell Mom, so she won't worry."

That was to be just the beginning.

Exactly two days after a second earthquake dream, the physical quake hit Siberia. Major. Then a third struck, exactly two days after a third dream.

Each big quake has its unique fingerprint, some rolling, some jarring, some undulating,—one jolt, two jolts, long, short. There was no mistaking it. In each dream, it was like being bodily shaken, going through the shock wave of the event itself. Usually it was the shaking that woke me, but during those few seconds, I would see glimpses of whatever was around me.

That, of course, was the dilemma, because except for the Anchorage quake, the maddening part was that I could describe it and know when it would happen, I just didn't know where. It was essentially useless information.

In that state of mind, one is willing to try anything. Since the events were so internal and intimate to me, I wondered if keeping it out of other people's consciousness could make a difference. So, when the fourth dream came, I decided not to tell anyone.

On my way to work two days later, I stopped for shaving cream, and staring me in the face, as I walked out, were the headlines, "Killer Quake Hits Japan." It's not easy to describe how one feels in that situation. I bought a paper. I still have it.

I didn't go to work. I went instead to Tracy's on Beachwood Drive and sat like a lump on the bar stool.

"What's the matter?" she asked. I showed her the paper.

There was an important message in all of it. The idea that someone is given prophetic powers so he can prevent the disaster from happening is marvelous fodder for "Psy-Fi" entertainment. But that's for people who have never been there. A true psychic event does not show you something that is not going to happen. That's the ultimate integrity of it.

Then what did it mean? What was the good of it? It certainly did not make me feel useful. Quite the opposite.

Then came the fifth. Then the sixth. Then the seventh. Then the eighth in a row, all major, each occurring exactly two days after the dream, and each exactly as I had seen it.

Then came the ninth. Then the tenth. And by this time about sixty people were asking to be called if I ever had a dream about Los Angeles.

It was the eleventh that finally brought home the real message, something totally different from anything I had been thinking.

In the eleventh dream I was in a moving boxcar with no seats, surrounded by swarthy people sitting on the floor. Many of them had hats and little colored wraps, both men and women. With a sudden jerk, we were thrown off the tracks. Next, I was looking down onto a mountain village with clay tile roofs, as the debris-filled torrents from a broken dam came slamming down the canyon upon it, tumbling and tumbling the whole village away, including all its inhabitants. Then I was at a hillside house with Spanish arches, where two women came running out, the owner and her housekeeper, as it still shook and cracked. Turning another direction, I witnessed a running blond woman suddenly crushed by a falling mass of stone or concrete. The detail was overwhelming.

When I got a call from brother John two days later, I knew what he was about to tell me. "Your dream is on the front of the L.A. Times," he said. "It was in Chile."

It was a fundamental lesson. It was not what I knew that was important. It is the fact that we are able to know things outside of time and space and trust them when they come to us. Eleven times in a row was enough. And upon that, the earthquake dreams stopped.

There were other dreams, of course, off and on—the Florence flood, the assassination attempt on Governor Wallace. But what is germane to this story is that I recognized without any doubt, that the dream of May 14th, although it went backwards instead of forward in time,—was the real thing.

4

The woman in black

No one in the Juana dream had seen me. I had come only as a disembodied messenger. That much seemed clear. But at the moment, I was too wired to deal with philosophical speculations.

What surprised me most was her appearance. I had always pictured her with black hair and small dark eyes. But she was not that at all. She was olive-skinned, with light brown eyes and really very pretty.

The night saw towering highs and wrenching lows. I sweated and blew puffs of air and paced the floor and talked to myself. I dressed for morning and waited for the sun to rise, and I was there at 7 AM when the doors opened at the UCLA Research Library.

A section on culture and travel was where I headed first, with its big slick picture books on landmarks and castles of Europe. Flanders was my guess. Though I had never been there or read its history, I recalled that it had been part of Philip's domain. So, that would make sense. Philip the handsome, Duke of Burgundy, he was heir to the Austrian throne.

Within twenty minutes I was staring at the very wall I had walked in the dream—four hundred and seventy-seven years ago! Nerve ends were wriggling all over me as I read it, "Summer palace of the early Dukes of Burgundy." Philip, of course, in its heyday, certainly would have gone there with his bride. It was in the district of Ghent.

Next, from the card catalogue, I checked out the few books that referenced Juana la loca or "Mad Joan," as she was known in England. There wasn't much. At the time I found only four pictures of her, and no two looked alike.

I had with me the sketches I had made, and it then occurred to me to drive my old junker over the hill to Universal Studios and pick the brains of an old friend. Wardrobe Department was a beehive, and coming unannounced I just handed him my sketch of her without comment.

"Oh, a period thing. You want it to look Dutch? 15th–16th Century?" he volunteered with no hesitation. "What is it, a play? But you can't use this. This is no good. Take one of my reference books. Just bring it back when you're done."

I left the studios without another word. The muscles in my legs wouldn't stop quivering on the seat of the old car all the way back to the office, where something even more startling was awaiting me.

The message light was flashing on the answering machine. It was Tracy.

"What the hell's going on over there?" she asked, almost sounding annoyed, "All morning long I've had this image on my mind, so strong I can't get rid of it.—It's a woman all in black, pacing back and forth in your office and tapping on your desk with a fan. She has something like a veil or lace over her head, so I never see her face. But she has beautiful hands.—Call me, sugar."

5

One can choose to avoid it or risk the unknown.
Either way, it is still there. So, what else is life
but to follow your soul?

The message shot a sizzle up the back of my neck. Then I realized I had not received my ritual greeting from the cat.

"Katangi?"

She was gone. Only minutes of searching finally found her bristling with adrenaline in a box under the work table. She pressed back with a warning growl, as I tried to coax her out, which brought on the icy feeling that she was reacting to something behind me.

It was no imagination. The cat knew it. Tracy knew it. I knew it. Something alien was present in my office. It hung in the air. I even ventured a look into the closet, as senseless as that might seem.

I didn't return Tracy's call. I needed to absorb the moment alone. If there is one signal trap to avoid, it is presumption—elaborating on the facts. I had repeated that lesson several times over.

During the years that brother John was living in Chicago, doing trade shows for I.B.M., Pfizer, Rockwell and whomever, I never got there in person. But I did visit him one night in a dream.

All the lights were off in his second floor apartment. It was the middle of the night, and I could just make out his face in the darkness. He was lying awake across the room on a bed, with his body angled out from the wall. In the moonlight outside a window to my right, I could see a weird old house, at least two stories tall.

"Do you do this all the time?" I asked.

"Yes," he answered.

Then I started across toward him. But something low and wide was blocking my way in the middle of the room. I had to walk around it,—to the left. I laid down behind him, looking back toward the direction I had come, when suddenly a man's voice from the neighboring house exclaimed, "Mother! It's blood!"

I was startled awake. "My God, it's blood!" I was thinking. Whatever it meant, it wasn't good. It disturbed me so much that I immediately got up and phoned him. No answer.

Of course, John was Consultant of Magic for the Smithsonian and always off to some distant location with the robots. So it wasn't unusual to find him away from home. I tried again in the morning.

Still no answer. Before starting anything else, I wrote down the whole dream, drew a diagram of the room and mailed it off at the corner mailbox. The phone was ringing when I got back to the office. It was John.

After I described it again on the phone, he said, "Well, it's not this place. There's no window on that wall, no big furniture in the middle of the room and no house like that next door. So it must be someplace else."

"Probably one of those crappy motels they make you stay in to save money," I laughed. "But anyway, when you see it, watch out!"

Two days later, he was on the phone again. "Have you ever seen the movie Psycho?" he asked?

"No," I said.

"Well, last night I was lying in bed, watching it on TV. Something was preempted and it came on about one in the morning. All at once, it shows the outside of the old Bates house, and Tony Perkins' voice says 'Mother, it's blood!' I said, 'That's it! That's Paul's dream.' I turned on the light and looked at your letter, which just arrived this morning, and there it was. The big thing in the middle of the room was my couch, pulled out into a bed. And the only way you can walk around it is to the left. Except, where you drew the window is my television. That's why I was lying angled-out, so I could watch the show."

"It had to be in black and white," I said, "because it looked just like bright moonlight."

"It was," he confirmed.

"Well, knock off the creepy movies," I said, "You're ruining my sleep." We laughed and hung up.

The lesson was, of course, that even with correct information you can still get it wrong. If I had taken more time to think about it, I would have realized that one could not be looking out a window at that old house from across the room.

I played Tracy's message again. It was important that I not read more into it than was actually there.

It was said that after Philip's death Juana wore nothing but black for the rest of her life. If the "woman in Black" was indeed Juana, then Tracy was not tapping into my dream of the beautiful young girl in Flanders. She was seeing something entirely different,—the ghost of a tragic old widow, the legendary prisoner of Tordesillas.

It was difficult to reconcile that the two were even the same person. Indeed, there was no evidence that they were. But the dream had blind-sided me. It was so intimate, so entrapping that even now it still held me hostage.

"There is a reason for everything," I kept reassuring myself, trying to eliminate the theatricality of it.

Being brought up in the home of a Sheriff's detective had also established a sequence in sorting things out. "First tell me what happened," Dad had drilled us a hundred times, "Then tell me how it happened. After that you can tell me why."

With the what and how already somewhat established, the main matter on my mind was now why. The idea of unfinished business had been an occasional topic in the family since childhood, stemming from dream-related incidents. They had involved all of us. And over time, we perceived that those kinds of events bore two threads in common: emotion and immediacy.

Crazy things flash through one's mind at a time like that. Stupid human rationalizing had stopped me from warning the innocent girl in her time of need. So what if she hadn't believed me? I could have told her anyway, important things. But I had done nothing.

Was I now being visited by the very horrors I had hoped to spare her in the dream? Was the old ghost now calling in its markers? As I say, crazy things go through your head.

I played the message a third time.

"—pacing back and forth—" The more I listened to it, the more the words rang of urgency, a plea for help. Instinct goaded me to do something. But what?

It was mention of my desk, the tapping on my desk, that drew it to focus, the big I.B.M. electric, with a page of the unfinished teleplay still in it.

"Of course!" I said aloud. "That's what I do."

First impulse shot me to the file drawers to retrieve the old folder that had lain untouched since the day I put it there. Partly typed, partly handwritten, its contents burgeoned with weird tales, dates, places—excerpts from the textbooks, along with pamphlets and little items from the trip. But even as my mind devoured them, their veil of seduction peeled back. It occurred to me, "What am I thinking?" That's all they were, a rehash of hand-me-down tales, dry reports, mementos, nothing one could recognize as a living breathing person. And all the time I was standing in the doorway of her own dimension: the woman in black, firsthand.

Sweeping the desk clean, I abandoned everything but my attention to the electric charge of the room. At that point, I really had no clue as to what was happening. It had the aura of schizophrenia. Not just two, but three moments in time were somehow converging, or so it seemed.

Katangi had the right idea. Had madness so altered the tragic queen that she was no longer the same person she had been? If the grisly tales were true, my visitor could be a psychopath, who opened her husband's coffin at night and made love to his bones. Whatever she was, I would respect it—for the moment.

As I rolled a blank page into the typewriter, switched it on and waited, my own paranoia swung like a compass-needle for assurance that the source of energy in my room was not lurking behind me.

Ten or fifteen minutes passed. In frustration, I got up to make sure the door was locked. I phoned brother John.

John had gone to work for Magical Productions as a designer of illusions about the time that I left there. He was in the middle of assembling a promotional robot, and my jingle brought him stepping over a mine-field of broken glass.

"Magical—so-to-speak," came the wry baritone greeting.

"Oh, no. Why?" I frowned.

"Typical," he said. "They just broke the big plate glass window in front to get out a shipping crate that they didn't bother to measure before they built it."

"And it has to be at the airport in forty-five minutes," I ventured, from past experience.

"Close," he droned. "Now I'm just waiting to hear that they drove off in the wrong truck. So, you were saying?"

John had enough on his hands, and I didn't get into it. "I'm not going to be answering the phone for a while," I told him.

"You all right?" he asked.

"Oh, yeah-yeah," I said. "I just didn't want to get interrupted for a while, and I thought maybe you'd let people know, so they won't get concerned."

"Soitenly," he said. "—All but our enemies."

I laughed and told him I would get back to him. He held the little tone generator up to the receiver and gave me a few R2D2 bleeps.

Even before I hung up, the photo on the wall of Meredith in her safari outfit was prompting me to make my second call. She had since moved into the big house in Bismarck and was there at home when I rang.

"Remember, what, four years ago, when you first called about going on the trip?" I reminded her, "The first thing you said was you heard I was going to Spain."

"Did I?" she mused.

"Yeah. I was just curious why it was you said that," I asked.

"Weren't you?" she seemed surprised.

"No," I told her. "I wasn't going anywhere."

"Well, then I don't know. It's a mystery," she chuckled. "How is little Katangi doing?"

"At the moment? Meditating," I said. I squatted down to see if I could pull her out of the box, while we chatted family-talk a few more minutes. But Katangi still spit at my hand, and the call revealed nothing.

By now it was lunchtime. The sounds of traffic funneled up the front stairwell from Weyburn Avenue, students on foray between classes, the hunger-rush into Hamburger Hamlet next door. At the electrologist across the hall, Rosamond's last patient of the morning was jabbering about her bathroom renovations and where she was headed to eat. In that unfavorable climate, I retreated to seclusion in my store room, where the stir of traffic was less disturbing. Not until about three in the afternoon did I return, the time when eyelids of the metropolis start getting heavy and students are back in class. I could concentrate again.

Katangi still had not budged. Some new messages were on the machine, but I did not listen to them. Sitting down again to the desk, I switched on the typewriter, leaned into it and let its hum relax me until the tension I had felt earlier subsided. Rather than simply sit there, and sensing no particular guidance, I began tapping out my own version of the crazy-queen tales from memory:

"—December of 1506. Where fog and blackness mingle, a lantern rises in the window of a lonely farm house. The old man rubs his eyes and strains to see what has wakened him: a glowing serpent of torches and droning chant, "Dirge, Domine, Deus, meus, in conspectu, tuo, viam, meum," the Office of the Dead. A funeral procession of hooded monks is passing like ghosts on the roadway. Their baggage, a great garish coffin, is draped in the Hapsburg colors, its golden hardware flickering in their firelight.

"The wife, now by his side, wraps herself in a blanket and scurries out into the field, where other peasants have also crept forth to spy.

"The rumors have sprung alive:—flapping robes, a pregnant woman all in black, the corpse of her rotting prince! Seized in its spell, they whisper the morbid gossip:

"—There she is—!"

"I told you, it's the queen!"

"We shouldn't be here. It's prying in God's affair—!"

"It's the same madness of her grandmother."

"She thinks her love can bring him back to life."

"—Refuses to give him up even to God—"

Suddenly, a flash inside my head brought teeth, flaring jets of steam, and the shrill blast of a giant black stallion only inches from my face. Its white-ringed eyes and the yelling of men sent me almost toppling over backward. It collapsed into oblivion as suddenly. But the shattering volume of it left numbing vibrations all over me. Bolting up and across the room, I slipped out into the hallway and leaned back against the wall, forcing myself to look calm. I guess it worked. A couple strolled by and nodded in greeting.

Whatever had just taken place, one thing was for certain. It was not of my own invention. As the surprise of it subsided and I was no worse for wear, I returned to the typewriter. This time I would be prepared. I resumed where I had left off:

"An old crone shrinks from the sound of creaking wheels beneath their royal burden, as it jostles over unseen pebbles and ruts, the concussion of its embalming perfumes violating her nostrils: "Ew! It's poisonous vapors—!"

"She has the wilderness in her eyes."

"He calls her from the casket."

Suddenly, launched by a cranky voice, "Madame, the village is overflowing—" the wraith of a strange bedroom began surrounding me like some reflection in a pane of window glass. There was a tall skinny man in papal robes, with sparse white hair.

It only lasted a few seconds then faded again. But something real had happened. I was just fearing it was lost, when came a house built right on a river bank. There was a noisy stirring on the road around me.

Oddly enough, it seemed that I could glance around, even though my eyes remained on the keyboard. At first I just typed impressions to remind myself: "Street crowd dust soldiers vendors/arguing/guns swords money wagons horses chickens flags jars trunks food dogs/lots of dogs/river grass—"

It was not like a trance. I knew when I had to change the paper. It was a matter of clinging to the activities that streamed past my senses.

I was on a road, partly cobblestone and partly dirt, that snaked parallel to the river and through an old town. Further away, more groups had set up camps down by the water, crowded-out by those who had arrived ahead of them. The din of barking, overstimulated children, fractious nobles, bleating sheep on the opposite hill and stamping horses mingled with the dust of more wagons still coming up the road on the other side of the water.

"You must do something to appease them," came the skinny man's voice again, addressing someone inside the nearby house. And there it came again, the bedroom. He was speaking to Juana.

Now twenty-eight, which I later deduced, she lay hollow-eyed and exhausted on an ordinary bed. "I've just given them a new Princess," was her sharp reply.

Her antagonist was none other than the seventy-four year old Cisneros Ximinez, Archbishop of Toledo. The most powerful Cardinal in Christiandom, he was second only to the Pope and no one to trifle with. His bony hands exhibited an intimidating crooked finger, as if it had once been broken and never properly healed.

"Simply convene the Court," he insisted. "I will bring together the best council of the land—"

"A council of my father's enemies, no doubt," she cut him off.

Neither would compromise and it rose in crescendo to an impasse. My fingers couldn't keep up with it.

That's the way it began.

I had no consciousness of time. But what did come of it were several remarks that she believed Philip had not died of natural causes. She was convinced he had been murdered. This was a jolt, because every history book attributes his death to an illness. Admittedly, that might be seen as a symptom of her paranoid mind. On the other hand, if true, it would throw a different light on everything that was transpiring.

When I had time to think about it, Philip's murder would not be so far-fetched. His arrogant behavior had antagonized the Spanish Court from the moment he arrived. Indeed, it had progressed to the point that he had estranged even Juana. Toward the end, she had taken up separate residence at the mayor's house in town.

Then another bit of a bombshell hit, regarding her ill-fated journey to Granada.

"It is dangerous. And what's more, it is fostering all kinds of outrageous gossip," I heard the old Archbishop barking.

"I know what they say," she sloughed it off.

"Do you?" he chided. "Can I put it more clearly?—And opening the coffin whenever you feel like it!"

"Oh. And how would it look to arrive in Granada with an empty casket?" she threw back. "Philip's men have already tried twice to steal the body. You know it."

His crooked finger hooked at the air, "Madame—"

Right then I knew. These were no dormant memories playing tricks. Never in any book was it ever mentioned that there had been attempts to steal the body and return it to Austria. Suddenly the common sense of it blew me away, the real reasons for opening the coffin. If it had been out of her sight for any length of time, she wanted to see for herself that the body was still there.

Nor was that to be the last revelation. Far more was happening here than I ever could have imagined.

"Oh, I've matters worse, so now I'm to do more?" her tactless retaliation insulted the old pontiff, and the argument jumped round and round. They were interrupted at times by the delivery of messages or various concerns for her comfort. Even though my typing had accelerated, I could not keep track of it all, and some of it ended-up looking like garbage.

It did not occur to me until later that the language they were speaking was any different from my own. At some point I became self-conscious of making verbal responses myself. It all seemed so spontaneous and real, without notice I became more and more involved in her world, while the Woman in Black was physically manifesting in mine.

6

*The Fox of Aragon arrives—a father's deceit—
strange documents—the garbled notes—a
postcard*

One can imagine moving holograms. At about ten in the evening, it started again. Flickers. Then came a large house with many rooms.

My sense was that it sat at the east end of some town, with wild vacant fields stretching into the distance beyond, brown and tinted pink with the low angle of the sun. "Sun is low," I typed. "—coming in through the front windows. The road, I believe, goes north, as far as can be seen. Cannot see the other direction. Table in the living room."

Suddenly there were people where none had been, gathered at a doorway. Before I could see it, I heard sobbing from beyond them. There, in a smaller room, Juana sat on a box in gasping sobs, pasty-white and deathly thin. About her, several others were hovering in anxiety. A maid servant kept squealing and wringing her hands, as an older lady shook her by the clothes and ordered her, "Water! A wet cloth!"

The man who had created the disturbance was Fernando. In leather riding clothes, he was accompanied by a soldier. "As God is my witness," he mumbled, "I had no idea—!"

He tried to lift Juana's chin, but she pulled away. He waved his soldier off to fetch something from his saddlebags.

"Please, my dear," he urged. "Give me your hand."

33

"Everything will be all right," the older woman kneeled beside her to calm and stroke her hair. I later determined that it was Lady Beatriz de Bobadilla, the powerful Marquessa de Moya of Segovia.

Juana could not speak, and Beatriz flashed the King an accusing glare that betrayed some historic acrimony between them.

"I didn't—No one told me she was so ill," he offered feebly.

"Well, now you know," the Marquessa snapped.

He switched subjects, "I hurried ahead of the others, to have a moment alone with her."

"Others? What others?" Beatriz rose up at him.

"Those perennial dukes. Dogging me all the way from the border," he hissed, again trying to lift his daughter to her feet.

"Well, get rid of them. She's too ill for this," Beatriz interceded to give Juana her own hand. "They can wait in town, until she's recovered."

The servant woman, Alicia, returned with the wet cloth—

I had no reference for the passage of time, until I happened to glance at my clock: a few minutes to midnight. Still the encounter dragged on, sometimes tediously. Juana refused to retire, as ill as she was. Her hands were shaking, and her eyes would not stop tearing.

Fernando was up to no good. At least, I detected that he was being devious. When they were alone, the discussions between him and Juana were testy. He forbade her to continue her journey to Granada with Philip's body. He claimed it would be an insult to her mother. Yet in blatant contradiction, he himself had already remarried.

My fingertips had become desensitized and I rubbed them across my lower teeth to restore the feeling, more and more often, as the devouring onslaught continued faster than I could keep up with it.

Finally, Juana grew so dizzy with the confrontation that Beatriz intervened and supported her away, somewhere into the rear rooms of the house. It was only after he was alone that I became sure of it: things were going all too well for Fernando.

According to Isabella's will, provision had been made that, if Juana was found incompetent or unwilling to rule, her father would rule in her place. And following the events I had just witnessed, the diabolical undercurrent seemed self-evident. It was Fernando, not Juana, who made sure that Philip's body was never buried. Tales of her macabre obsession with the corpse would be believed. It laid bare all the marks of an arch-villain. Provoking her into such a wretched state of emotion played convincingly into the illusion of her incompetence. Whatever else has been said of Juana, two things were never in dispute. From earliest childhood, she was known as a protégé, a wizard in math, a linguist, brilliant, talented, outspoken and opinionated. It made her a dangerous adversary, except to those whom she loved. She loved too hard. And she adored her father.

In the books Fernando was not called the Fox of Aragon for nothing. His double-dealings are legendary. He had even made a secret pact with Philip behind Juana's back while she was answering to a contentious government in his protracted absence.

So, when Townsend-Miller suggests that he probably chose Juana's weakest moment and woke her in the middle of the night for her signature, it is quite plausible. Fernando's self-styled document gave him sweeping control over all of Juana's affairs, even down to her personal household and place of residence. But with Philip dead, she had to trust someone. Who else was there?

As the waves of writings overlapped on into the morning, an amazing dichotomy was rising between the events I was witnessing and their recorded counterparts.

<u>From the textbooks</u>:

Though she was Queen of the empire, Juana complied with her father's wishes, until Philip's body had lain unburied for two and a half years. In frustration, she notified him that she was beginning to make her own plans. Suddenly, on February 14th, 1509, while the town slumbered under a blanket of ice, Juana was wakened at 3 A.M. by a band of Fernando's soldiers. When the sun arose, the whole house was found vacant.

The Queen's continuing deterioration was her father's most painful tragedy, and he moved her to the tranquility of the countryside. Her new residence was to be the castle of Tordesillas. On the remote central plains he kept watch over her sad decline in privacy for the next eight years.

That Juana was content to languish in stagnation for nearly a decade was proof of her incompetence. The chilling stories leaked out that she sat in darkness for days and refused to speak at all, that she ate her meals on the floor and constantly passed water.

Whenever she wished, she was allowed to visit Philip's coffin at the monastery of Santa Clara, which was only a short walk away. It seemed to calm her. But as time passed, even that seemed to disappear from her thoughts. Eventually, none but her keepers were allowed to see her.

<u>Westwood</u>:

Wednesday was already showing its face, and I had not left my desk. The writings had become like the runner's high, as if one is outside his body, running alongside himself. Only something puzzling and unexpected would have grounded me again from that stream of consciousness. And it came for the first time that night. Suddenly it was just like the dreams. With my body still on remote at the desk, I found myself walking about the castle.

Surrounding me in peripheral images arose an austere stone chamber with beam ceilings and a bank of tall windows on one side. I assumed it to be an upper chamber of the old fortress at Tordesillas. At the far end of the room was the marble figure of a woman saint, about five feet tall on a pedestal, which stood at a strange place, away from the wall. One could walk all around it. The rest of the room was fairly clear of furniture, except for some chairs and the table where Juana was sitting. There were no sounds. She was alone.

In front of her lay many documents—formal legal documents. Some were stacked open to her left. Others were already folded with wax seals, and she was putting her signature to another of them. I could determine no particular expression on her face.

I couldn't put a finger on it, but I had the uncomfortable feeling that something was amiss.

"If these documents are important enough to require her signature as well as Fernando's," I labored, "why is someone not overseeing this?"

Nor did she look unhealthy as I had expected. She was quite focused on what she was doing. In other words, where was Fernando? Where was anybody, for that matter?

There was no explanation. My eyes were getting blurry. I needed to shut down for a few minutes, and I remember nothing past that.

It was the clattering of mail coming through the slot in the door, which caused me to open my eyes. I was lying on the floor exhausted, with bright mid-morning sunlight streaming in through the window over my desk.

A whole ream of typed pages was strewn about everywhere. The bizarre remains of seventeen hours of typing brought my breathing shallow. It was familiar, of course, except in panorama. That startled me.

I picked up one of the nearest pages to see what it said: *"you msut be tuireed from your endlesss travels/d9o I dewtect a l.ittle rerprin?/hope so./sp, lkt is my haughty littl princeqssafter all/its the best I could fsso on such short motice/Oh juyana fdon't continues tro chATSISE ME. srace. how mucg mUst I appolol ZE/iLL DECIDEE THAt come. yOU MUst see yr nu graNDDATER Ill awake her/plesa don['t put weqme off asos abryuptly/I understa d youe've already rermaRRIES/S we begion with that, do ee?/and a niece of Louis/Juana lerts'talk about now/you can do as zsy see fit until I return from Gran sada/now listen to yopurm father/Don't cOonfortnt me please/it would be n insult to hunon Philip your amother/That si kjy affair fatther/I wil tell you whaern it is toe to burty Philip—dizzy. noises—what?/oh tgreacherous cvultures/who/don't assk pests Never mionsds/Give me a moment I'll berihdbnfc/You wil notxx wl gostraight to bed/Im not,mthinking very well./thats what your fREHRE is here fofr, chils. my how thingas do change.—rush hjer out—a soldier—"*

"Christ Almighty," I groaned. "I have to rewrite everything, or I won't even remember what it says." More exasperating, nothing was numbered.

The heavy presence in the room was gone, and I rolled over to find Katangi watching me from the file cabinet.

"No smart-lip," I warned. "This isn't funny."

My skin felt salty and my shoulders were stiff. I started a new pot of coffee, pulled off my shirt, ran water over my head, rinsed my armpits then gathered up the fallen pages, while I toweled down.

As I came to it, I also scooped up the mail from the carpet and pitched it onto the table. Then something subliminal drew me back to it,—the edge of a postcard. I pulled it out. It was the picture of an old greenish tapestry, the classic kind one finds in a museum. Its two main figures were a young nobleman on the left, with his hand out to a young noble woman on the right. Her feet were in the air behind her, as if she were dancing, and a yellow scarf covered her hair.

A thud hit my chest, as I turned it over: "The centerpiece of the exhibit," its caption announced, "A rare Flemish tapestry, depicting Philip of Austria and Juana of Castile."

7

*Wednesday: Jeryll—Miss Charlotte—Miraflores—
the documents and high treason—the
dimensions keep growing*

Postmarked eight hours before the dream, the card sported a generic address-o-graph label and announced some art exhibit in Phoenix, Arizona. How did I even get on the mailing list? What were the odds against that? Astronomical.

I had to talk to someone.

Mystery novelist and friend, Jeryll Taylor had the office next door. The best of everything the 60's and 70's had to offer, she had somehow pulled idealism and practicality together into one place without burning down the garage. Jeryll would be an ideal sounding board. Besides, she already knew Meredith and Tracy. I gave our special signal-knock on the north wall, and she returned the "okay."

Her big golden retriever met me at the door with three tennis balls in his mouth. "Hi, Frodo. Is your mom home?" I asked.

"Come in," she called from her desk.

Jeryll's walls were a synopsis of the world, with posters and photos of ships, a sunrise, Lenny Bruce, ancient artifacts, Art Buchwald, jazz artists, the Taj Mahal and eclectic mementos.

"I came by earlier, but you didn't answer my tap," she said, offering me a bag from Stan's Donut Shop, "on the way back from the tennis courts, where Frodo discovered that he can

40

now carry three balls at the same time. I'm toying with the idea of renting him to the pawn shop. What do you think?"

It was awkward. I didn't know where to start, so I just let her do the talking for a minute.

Eying a broken half-donut in the bottom of the bag, I made a face, to which she countered, "It's perfectly justifiable. I poured too much coffee, and it was the only way it would come out even....You seem to be taking this rather badly."

I handed her the postcard. There was a hang-fire, while she read it then looked up. I began spewing the whole thing out from the beginning.

"Well," she finally mused. "That explains it."

That my subconscious noises had been loud enough to be heard through the walls was mortifying. Obviously I had been more immersed in the visions than was comfortable to admit.

"I thought you were having another tiff with your agent," she smirked, "But now that I know it's only a deranged ghost from the Inquisition, I can put my mind to rest."

"The point is, no one can claim this is just in my head," I took back the postcard. "A physical thing coming right through my door into the office?—Oh, jeeze."

"What?"

A dormant recollection was surfacing, something that hadn't occurred to me at all, until just now. "Barcelona," I said. "I've had TWO free trips to Spain, not just one. My midshipman cruise."

"So?" she elicited, "You think that means—?"

"I'm just saying—eight years ago," the thoughts rambled on mute in my head. But as it all began coming back, I realized that Barcelona, too, had been notably strange.

I had barely stepped ashore with some buddies, when one of them started looking for a place to buy cigarettes.

"There's a little tobacco store right around the corner," I had said, without thinking. And there it was, a big cigar sign hanging over the sidewalk, right around the corner.

"Oh, you've been here before, you fart-head," they accused me and thought I was playing a joke when the same thing happened a few more times.

"Look, I'm not the C.I.A.," Jeryll offered, "but if you want my opinion, go to a movie. Get it off your mind."

"—Off my mind?" I scoffed, "I can practically feel her vibrations right now through the wall."

"How rude of you to go and say that!" she assumed a mischievous pose, "Now, I'll have to pull back all my furniture." Reverting to the tea, she went on, "If you want to know what I think, it's simple. Any woman could tell you."

I waited.

"Elementary. It's a female thing," she arched a brow of fundamental truth, "Juana has an agenda. And you're the patsy."

"A—," I coughed, "I knew I could count on you to bolster my confidence."

"I hate to say it," she continued, "but this does not sound like something you should be fooling around with, Paul Casey. Face it, la loca means crazy. The woman was insane. And trust me, if someone all the way across town, like Tracy, can see a mad woman prowling around your office, tapping on your desk with a fan, it's not a game. It could even be dangerous. It could make you—"

"Crazy-er?" I finished.

An implacable hum said it all. But as I was leaving, she added, "—And any more of this creepy stuff, Frodo and I better get the first report, or no more artistic donuts for you."

It was nice to end on a chuckle, but the affair had risen to a new dimension. What else may have been going on in my life I was soon to find out. Something even more extraordinary was already on its way.

Returning to my office, I locked the door and poked the postcard between some books to get it out of sight. The ringer was off, but I could see that a new call was coming in on the phone, and I picked it up by reflex. The woman's voice had a foreign accent, someone calling herself Miss Charlotte.

She was Charlotte Zutram, who said she got my name from Franklin Lacey, as a possible screenwriter for a film she wanted to produce. My great friend, Franklin was co-author of The Music Man. I told her I'd call her back when I finished what I was doing.

But Miss Charlotte was so enthusiastic I bore with her and let her explain the project, which was the life story of Ignacio de Loyola, to star Jim Bailey, the nightclub performer.

"I can come to your office," she said.

"No," I tried to curtail the conversation, while I took out a pen to write her number. "I'll have to get back to you."

"I'm willing to pay you some front money," she went right on. "I don't have a lot, but—"

"Miss Charlotte," I interrupted as gently as possible, "If Franklin referred you, I'd be more than happy to get together, as soon as I've finished what I'm doing right now. Just give me—"

"I have already done the research—" she continued.

"Miss Charlotte, give me your phone number. Okay?" I finally got her stopped.

That settled, I took a moment to scan the pages I had already written. They were a mess. Yet as disturbing as it had become, Juana's encroaching disaster seemed mine as well, because it continued to surprise and horrify me. More to the point, I was haunted by her face. There was really no hesitancy. I had to continue.

I threw a T-shirt over the answering machine to mask its blinking light, drew the shade behind me to lessen the effects of morning in Westwood, took a series of slow deep breaths and sat before the typewriter. Closing my eyes, I invited back that sense-memory connection, which had siphoned me away before, through its crevice in time.

After a minute, Katangi vanished again under the table. I got caught up in watching for some evidence of the enigmatic ghost to appear, perchance to glimpse her features that were masked even in Tracy's visions. But it only delayed things.

Finally, the words and images began filtering through again. This time it brought a wave of euphoria. It was a room where I had actually stood in my own lifetime. There was a photo of it on the wall.

It was the Monastery of Miraflores. Its wellspring of grisly tales and chilling intrigues was the reason Meredith and I had visited it. But unlike the picture I had taken, there now stood the coffin, lying in state before the altar. The chapel was deserted, its wooden pews smelling of soap.

I marveled, "This is not from memory!" The smell was new, not as I had experienced it in person, but a room freshly scrubbed. To one side of the altar was a small table covered by a lace runner upon which sat a silver bowl. Nor were the pews the same, either. They were heavier, elaborately carved and lined with cushions, not the simple benches that stand in their place today.

After his Requiem Mass, Juana had moved Philip's body to Miraflores for safekeeping, under twenty-four hour guard. Here it was, where the legends were spawned that she was so jealous of Philip she would allow no women near the dead body.

My exhilaration at the familiar surroundings, I suppose, made it indistinguishable from real time: spookily, almost without sound, the door is swung open by the guards in the yard outside, and Juana enters alone. She waits until the door is closed, before continuing on, where anguish overcomes her again. She places a hand upon the coffin above the place of her Prince's head.

"What fatal calamity is upon us? What enemy, whose name no one will speak? I find eyes in every shadow—!" she withdraws her hand. "Oh, my God, where is Fernando? Whom can I trust? No one..."

Her piteous "eyes in every shadow" set off a self-conscious alarm that I hardly dare breathe, lest it somehow frighten her. But a grizzled head suddenly rising from the rear of the altar vanquishes all else, where appears a grey-bearded old monk. It is he, who is responsible for the smell of soap.

Perhaps it is his solitary demeanor, but I immediately know who he is—the famous old Hermit of Burgos. He kneels, but she motions him up.

"I have heard of you. The Holy One," she says. "That you speak to no man, except through the mind."

He makes no answer.

"If God has sent you, then you know my grief. They also say that you travel without need of the body. If this is so, then I charge you to teach me the wisdom of these crafts," her voice trails, almost to pleading. "While I wait for my father, I will come to you each day, here at Miraflores."

That instant it struck me. All those bizarre tales spun right into place like a chain reaction. He was the legendary monk of Miraflores that all the stories referred to. But what nobody had ever put together was what happened fifteen years later, a phenomenon in the Room Without Light.

The practice of astral-projection reached its zenith among the Spanish monks of her very day. And who was the old Hermit of Burgos, but a leader of the astral-projection cult.

Now this is the fascinating connection. By the time Juana was forty-four, she had been locked away in the room without light for years, having no contact at all with the outside world. Suddenly she threw her keepers into a panic by telling them all kinds of things she could not possibly know,—places they had gone, meetings that had been held, exact dates, even things that were said.

"She talks to the stones!" her keepers exclaimed in high alarm. "There has to be a traitor in the castle! An informant!" It was the only thing they could imagine. These records we know from the suspects who were actually interrogated.

But since security was air-tight over the entire town, and purging all the guards did not stop it, what other explanation was there?

Tales of the old mortuary cult say that a monk of Miraflores told Juana of a king who was dead for years, then came back to life. That was the reason, they claimed, that she wandered about with the rotting corpse, waiting for him to come back to life. But as my pages kept falling to the floor, more and more it loomed as an insidious propaganda campaign. Of course, it was the hermit they were talking about. Whoever started the rumors had to know that.

Juana suspected murder for excellent reason. Philip had harvested enemies by the battalion. But prying no answers from the physicians, she did what anyone might do. She turned to the mystic. And if there is anything consistently known of Juana, it is that she seemed to learn almost anything without effort.

Yet at the same time, that was another thing which never made sense. How could she be so bright and so gullible at the same time?

In the rare moments that I surfaced to think, the dominos continued falling. The story crossing my typewriter bore no resemblance to the old legends at all. Even the legitimate records began taking on new colors.

If Philip's public philandering and dealings behind her back were not humiliating enough, the final straw must certainly have been his outrageous declaration of war on Segovia. Leading a Flemish army, he began the march to seize its citadel and divide the spoils among his comrades. Segovia was not only Castilian, it was the ancestral home of Juana's close family friends and Beatriz herself.

There were many accounts of it, all telling the same thing. Juana had erupted in rage and single-handedly delayed his entire army for days in the wild fields along the road.

"No," I decided, "They were not even living together at the time his fatal illness struck. This is not a woman who would go insane over his loss."

It was not obsession that drove her. Juana was Spanish. She loved her people. She had brought the arrogant power-hungry prince to Spain in their marriage and was obligated to see the disaster put to its final rest.

Wednesday was an endless shrapnel of grievances, often people without names or sequence. I simply typed it. But along about the wee hours of May 16th, something else began to unravel. It was that most pernicious question. If Juana was not insane, why would she agree to remain incommunicado for those eight long years that Fernando kept her there?

It was upon the reappearance of the room at Tordesillas, that I realized what had struck me wrong the first time. It was much the same as before, except that Juana was now composing a letter, apparently to her father. It was the documents themselves.

The documents! They were all composed in the same pen as her letter. Side-by-side, it was unmistakable. She was not simply signing them, she had authored the entire lot! Juana believed she was actively involved in the governmental processes. Yet there is no record of such documents anywhere.

This was the big bombshell.

Juana only knew what she was told by her father, which means that all of his reports to the Court were lies. The damaging gossip to discredit her was not only intentional, it was orchestrated by the Fox of Aragon himself. He sacrificed his own daughter to personal ambition. It was treason.

My flare of excitement whipped quickly into anger, watching as if an old horror film from which one cannot disengage. Even more heart-wrenching was to witness the care she was taking in her petition to the despicable father who had betrayed her. Tears flooded my eyes.

It woke me to my physical exhaustion. I ceased typing. In the bright shallow glare of the desk lamp, I worked the muscles in my back and neck. I had not turned on the overheads. The room was still full of strange energy. I got up and walked about. I talked to myself aloud. Katangi was still under the table.

By 1516, Fernando had grown as useless to the Court as Juana. He had taken to traveling in disguise, consorting with sorcerers and soothsayers in a vain attempt to sire a new male heir. But his treachery had led him into quicksand, for Juana stood to inherit his kingdom of Aragon, also. Her true condition certainly would be revealed upon his death.

With Castile again in disarray, the Archbishop of Toledo finally forced an audience with Juana, to determine her state of mind for himself. This is what I was thinking about,—and the record of their findings.

The emissary spoke with Juana for three days, and returned with the report that she seemed to be completely lucid. However, their assessment was inconclusive, because she had the absurd delusion that she was ruling the empire from Tordesillas.

Absurd? It was precisely the payoff of her father's device to placate her. But treachery takes its own captives. Fernando was accelerating toward a messy end. He wrote a new will bypassing Juana and naming her younger son as his legitimate heir to the Kingdom of Aragon.

Instant backlash erupted in Castile, for this would divide Spain in two and jeopardize their position as the dominant world power. An entourage set out determined to track him down and coerce him into rescinding his will. They caught up with him as he lay dying at a lonely little camp in the hills. By now, too weak to fight, Fernando perpetrated his ultimate betrayal. In exchange for rescinding the will, he extorted their oath that they would not tell Juana when he died. As inconceivable as it seems, they agreed.

On that dry stony hillside the death-knell sounded for the freedom of a queen and altered the course of history forever.

I spoke again to the air, "What am I supposed to do?" "But there came no answer, only that same eerie sense of someone there.

By now a three-day beard was my only clock. Time did not seem to matter. The pages kept coming and coming. The images kept shifting and shifting, streaking toward her destruction, when a ripple of strings shook me back again into the Twentieth Century. The guitar. It was the same guitar I had seen in the vault at Tordesillas!...—Sitting upon a bedspread of dark wine-color,—Juana, playing such as one might expect to hear at Carnegie Hall.—Now a girl from my left, dancing to the music. Catalina! My god. Catalina!"....

Willowy blonde, she could have been the princess of every fairytale. Born in a farm house and raised in the awful old fortress, the future Queen of Portugal was probably the only joy in Juana's life. Every motion of the girl reflected it in her face.

The princess teased her mother to dance with her, until finally she rose to her feet, still playing for the two of them without missing a beat. It was so transfixing that I found myself frozen, just watching. The girl looked about ten, and I turned back to the keyboard to bang it out: "Catalina, 10 yrs old. Dancing. Guitar-Juana. Prob 8 yrs at Tordesillas.."

Knock-knock, knock-knock-knock!.... Everything collapsed again into Thursday morning. Westwood.

Standing outside the clouded glass of my door was a woman holding a big brown book, as best I could tell. I played 'possum. But she had already heard the typing, I suppose, because she knocked again and did not leave.

Since the spell was broken anyway, I ran my fingers through my hair and went to answer it, "Yes?"

"Paul? We spoke on the phone," she started.

Her hair was long and blondish. I put her in her mid-sixties. She spoke with a foreign accent and exuded a powerful energy. "Charlotte," I said.

The short version was that she had borrowed a rare biography of Ignacio de Loyola from a friend at the Archdiocese and wasn't supposed to have it.

"I know you're busy, but this won't take long," she started to open the giant volume as she stepped in. "It's just that I have to return this book today, or I'll get my friend in trouble. And it mentions something that I didn't find in any other source."

"If you just xerox it, you can return it, then we'll have plenty of time later—" I tried to be civil.

But she went right on, "It's almost noon. You have to eat sometime. Let me take you to lunch. Alice's Restaurant is right down the street."

So it was, almost noon. The ogre in the mirror confirmed it. But my appearance left Miss Charlotte undaunted, and just the mention of food set my stomach growling. It seemed the quickest way to both ends, so off we went.

I liked her. Miss Charlotte was flying a pipedream, I thought. Jim Bailey was a popular female impersonator, not a film star. But he was her friend, and somehow they both were convinced that he looked exactly like Ignacio. That seemed to be the basis of the whole project.

Anyway, it was true, she had done a great deal of research. The least I could do was reward her with my attention, and we waited for a table where we could talk in private.

"I've read everything I could find, and this is the only romantic thing ever mentioned in his life," she cracked the huge volume. "But I think we've really hit upon something. The forbidden love affair! Imagine how that could be developed for the movie, the driving force that ultimately brought him to dedicate his life to God. It's made for a movie."

I expected a chapter or a few pages at least, but as she opened to a marker and turned the book for me to read, the whole phenomenon literally paralyzed my speech. The single thing she had come to show me out of that massive biography was a tiny footnote in fine print at the bottom of a page. It summarized an incident at Court, where Ignacio had been introduced to the twelve-year-old Princess Catalina, a daughter of Queen Juana the First of Spain.

"The second he laid eyes on her, he fell madly in love and never recovered from it—" Charlotte's voice was no longer at the table. It was coming from the moon. Charlotte, the restaurant, the book were just wallpaper, wallpaper of an incredible wormhole that had somehow touched down in my life. Her visit was never about a screenplay. That would never happen. She had come to certify the names still fresh on my typewriter: not merely one, but Catalina and Juana both.

Excusing myself as politely as possible, I could think of nothing but getting back to my office—and the Woman in Black.

8

Neptune—a strange prophecy—arrival of the Hapsburgs—more unanswered questions.

If the postcard was a sign, then Charlotte's unscheduled appearance was a billboard. The top of my skull answered every step on the pavement. On the sunlit streets of the buzzing village came a biting moment of truth. I was addicted. I could no longer leave it alone. More candidly, I could no longer leave Juana alone.

It was a classic metaphor, the struggle of life against death. But upon the miniature stage of my office it had polarized into two main combatants. Juana was fighting to stay afloat in a maelstrom of power-mongers, while swimming toward her was her carnivorous destiny played by the Woman in Black.

My front stairs opened directly onto Weyburn Avenue, only forty feet from the Bruin Theater. So on weekends, the ticket lines often extended past the door. And as I approached the entrance, yet another odd recollection popped to mind. It had been Halloween night, 1970. I remember the date, because some of the people were in costume for the evening.

It was late, probably about ten-thirty or eleven. I had started out alone for dinner at the Good Earth, and as I edged through the line, I heard, "You, Sagittarian."

Well, that's enough to delay a Sagittarian for a moment or two, and I turned to find a young man addressing me.

"Yes, you," he had said, "I'm sorry. I don't know why I'm telling you this, but Neptune is about to go direct in Sagittarius for the next fourteen years. I just thought you ought to be aware of it."

"Fourteen years?" I kibitzed back, "Would you believe that guy? He never knows when to leave, never pays for a thing."

"Seriously," he insisted, "it's going to be a heavy time for you. You're going to know things. Things you don't even want to know."

"Oh, no, it's already starting," I laughed.

I thanked him and went on to dinner. I never saw the man again. But that flash memory now seemed to plug into the growing circuitry. "By God," I realized, "Meredith had called in early November, not more than a week later, with that unexplained remark about Spain." Was there really something to the horoscope connection?

As for Neptune, that, too, would raise its head again in an even more astonishing way, in my upcoming encounter with the BIRTH CARDS. But meantime, there is more to tell.

It was still about noon. The writings began very quickly this time and engulfed me more directly than before.

All conscious time evaporates when one straddles a dual reality. Everything is perceived in process. Scenes played in and out, as their pages fed through under the hammers on the carriage. But at some point, whenever, an alarm went off in my head. It was the sound of a name, a name I recognized, Guillaume de Chievres.

"Chievres-Chievres," I recalled from the Townsend-Miller book. "—The Hapsburgs are in the castle!"

Oh, my God. This was it! This was the moment, the agony of my dream, the horror of which I had wanted so desperately to warn her—the point of no return!

The Flemish envoy, including her teenage son Charles, had rushed immediately for Tordesillas, upon news of Fernando's death. It was a thinly veiled attempt to reconcile the bad blood they had generated between the Austrians and Juana. Now, of course, the winds of fate had reversed all that. A second kingdom had passed into her hands. It was the first time in three hundred years that all of Spain fell under a single scepter. It all belonged to Juana, and the Hapsburgs had some fancy fence-mending to do.

Twelve years earlier, her turbulent separation from the three eldest children in Austria had been almost a replay of the notorious five-day standoff between Juana and her mother at La Mota. In a test of wills between the old Queen and the Queen-to-be, Juana had been publicly arrested at the city gates and bodily carried away by soldiers for attempting to take her second son back with her to Austria.

Now, because of Fernando's treachery, the almost unbelievable situation existed. Juana could have left Tordesillas at any time, and no one would have dared to stop her. But she didn't know it.

That is what the Flemish envoy was about to discover, and it had me in contortions on the edge of my chair. Here are some notes, which were later retyped: "...One of Fernando's henchmen, keeper of the castle is bowing in the doorway. It is night, an electrical storm brewing. It is not the gallery, but a suite of rooms with windows also looking out over the river. 'The Lord Guillaume de Chievres, Your Majesty,' the man says and backs out.

"The Flemish nobleman enters and bows. The room is very dark, with only one candelabra glowing at the sideboard beneath a large tapestry portraying a stag hunt. Eyes of the hunters can be seen in its weave, an arrow in the neck of the deer, but not much else."

At first I cannot see Juana at all, for she sits in a large chair in dense shadow. He does not see her at first, either. She remains as still as a sphinx. It is plain that they have a previous acquaintance, and not a pleasant one.

"Your Majesty—!" he says, as his eyes find her. "Please, forgive Ferrer. It was entirely at my insistence."

There is no indication that she has even heard him.

"—With all the disturbing reports about your illness," he goes on, "I felt it my first duty in Spain to offer you whatever assistance I may."

In the stillness, his own voice seems particularly loud, and his discomfort shows in the small movements of his fingers. "—Especially at this sad time..." he adds. Needing something to fill the void, he glances around. "Well—! May I..?"

Straining to sound cheerful, the nobleman ventures over to the candelabra for a flame to light more candles. "Of course, by the time news reaches Austria, it's—" A blinding bolt of lightning intervenes, framing her, and he almost forgets what he is saying, "—always exaggerated."

Suddenly, the wild tales do not seem exaggerated, and he mutters on, "—The workings of politics..."

"Good health never makes good gossip." He almost jumps at the sound of her voice. "Bluntly," she adds, "I find your visit quite a curiosity. What lure of profit has attracted you to Tordesillas?"

"What? Oh, Your Majesty. A jest," he shifts nervously and concentrates on lighting the candles.

"You haven't seen it in the daylight," she drops an aside.

Grasping at the tone of humor, he regains some confidence, "You haven't changed, I'm pleased to see."

"Not my distaste for nonsense," she replies.

"Exactly," he frowns. "That's the puzzle. I mean, why do you continue in this morbid place? It's not like you at all."

For the first time, she stirs, as if thinking the same thing. She stands to reveal her straight black gown and a black shawl about her shoulders with glossy threads of color woven into its borders. "My father could better answer that," she muses. "He is quite fluent in excuses."

At the remark, Chievres does a double-take. It is this exact moment, I am thinking, that the whole history of the western world is altered forever.

Had Juana regained her throne, no foreign usurpers would have looted her treasuries, conscripted the Spanish youth for wars they knew nothing about or diverted her gold from the new world to Austrian celebrations and excesses. Spain would have remained the world's greatest power on land and sea, for above all else, Juana loved her people. And they well knew it.

Not only might the entire Western hemisphere be Spanish-speaking today, but in actual fact, there might never have been an Elizabeth of England, for Catherine of Aragon was Juana's sister. And therein lies an anecdote worth telling. She had just set sail to receive the Crown of Castile in 1504.

Openly wounded by the forced separation from her three eldest children, Juana ordered a sudden surprise detour to England, where she vented her fury upon the beleaguered young Henry, over his abuse of her little sister. So fierce was her diatribe that Henry fled and barricaded himself in his private chambers, refusing to venture out again, until assured that the witch was again far out at sea. All the more humiliating for a Prince of Wales, she delivered it in impeccable English.

In those days, England was still only a small island, struggling with the Celts of Ireland. Conversely, Juana had the power and the means to do anything she wanted. And Henry bore the scars of it. To press the point, she even named her last child Catalina in honor of her unhappy sister, Catherine. Had Juana assumed control of her throne, it is unlikely that Henry would have risked her wrath again.

But her most sweeping impact might well have been the forgotten fact that nearly five centuries ago, Juana the First of Spain launched a revolutionary new government "by the people and for the people." Though sadly short-lived, it was a democracy that spanned half the planet from pole to pole, the first of its kind in the western hemisphere. Just imagine.

Thursday, as these things tumbled through my mind, I felt sticky, contaminated, contaminated by the crime scene of where it all had happened, where history was about to suffer a cold-blooded disfigurement all over again, —Tordesillas, 1517, and the arrival of the Hapsburg Prince.....

"Fernando has his own reasons," Juana breathes, her mind straying elsewhere for a second.

Chievres stiffens slightly, going on silent alert, as if detecting something diabolical. His eyes wander around and come to rest on the documents.

"He's noticed them!" I tightened almost without breath.

While the Fleming makes small talk, he passes by the table for a closer look.

History portrays the Queen as idle, simple and pathetic. But there was no shred of such a woman before me. It was treachery improvising on its feet. Her misinformation was all the weakness he needed.

My fingers began almost mindlessly on the keys, as if I were drifting apart from it. I wanted to shove him,—hit him.

Making sure she is watching, Chievres takes a second stroll past the table, then halts and goes back, as if spying it for the first time. He glances to her, then back to the documents. She finds his behavior inexplicable.

"My god.. We must get you out of here—!" he retracts with a mask of horror.

"Chievres,—" she starts.

"Tonight. Before they can stop us!" he paces about, thinking fast. "Your Majesty,—" he darts to the door and swings it back, "His Imperial Highness, the Prince Charles, your son, Madame."

Juana goes rigid and pale, as a peach-cheeked teenager steps in and snaps a military bow. Her dead husband's features are so mimicked in his face that it jars her. Impassioned, she rises up toward him, but the boy reverts to rapid chattering, a stilted speech: "My dear Queen and mother, it seems a lifetime since we said good-bye in Flanders, but the choice was not then ours, and I have lived in the constant ambition to be reunited again, as we rightfully belong. The news of your long illness has grieved me greatly, but—"

Pained by the terror in his face, Juana extends her hand, but it only throws the adolescent boy into further panic and faster rattling: "—but I hope that our presence here will bring you aid and comfort,—that we may be of some small service, in whatever way you may desire—"

I knocked my cold coffee off onto the floor. I didn't look to see where it went. The boy was breaking into a dripping sweat, and from the torment of Juana's expression, she must have recognized the ruthless brainwashing her child had undergone at the hands of his mentors. Perhaps she even feared the triggering of his past epileptic seizures.

"It is with sincere devotion that I humbly present myself to you.—Your servant, Madame.." Charles genuflects and withdraws a very large stiff step, avoiding her eyes.

Juana gives Chievres a grievous look, but he dismisses it without notice, "Would you recognize him, Your Majesty?"

She turns softly to her son, "My, look at the years that can never be returned to me. How you do please me, Charles. The thousands of times I've imagined this meeting—"

"Madame, if I may—" Chievres interrupts.

"Forgive me, Guillaume. I will find some way to reward you," she moves gently to the petrified boy, "It was not nearly enough.."

"But all is done! Don't you see?" Chievres shatters the reverie. "Quickly, before we're found out. Before they stop us!"

Juana frowns. Chievres indicates "Charles," then motions the young Prince out of the room. The boy is only too eager and gone before she can stop him.

"What are you talking about?" she asks.

"I didn't want to say it in front of His Most Esteemed Excellency," Chievres whispers urgently.

"What are you talking about?" she repeats.

"This! These!" he seizes some of the documents from the table, and she freezes in perplexity.

He looks appalled, "How could anyone miss it? They mean nothing! Papers!"—

Juana charges at him, "Get your hands off those—!"

"Don't you comprehend it? You're doing nothing here! It's all a trick. They're claiming you're insane, for God's sake!" he glances around the room, "—This,—"

Juana snatches the documents back with a chill, "Get out of here. Get out I said."

"Imperial Seal," he gapes, "It's counterfeit, a fraud, to keep you pacified! These seals are counterfeit! I can prove it. But first we must get you out of here!"

"What are you proposing?" she demands.

"It's obvious," he throws up his hands. "Obvious. Your natural heir, trained and schooled by the best—"

"What are you proposing?" she cuts him short.

"A simple contract, a few witnesses,—" he begins.

"I'm not signing anything," she retaliates.

"—transferring Fernando's powers to your son," he exclaims. "To assist you, by your side—"

"Tell me of my son," she changes the subject. "Does he still suffer the seizures?"

Juana—" Chievres forgets himself and quickly makes apology, "Your Majesty.. At times, but he's grown out of the worst of it. And capable. He has your wit."

"I see," she turns away.

He pursues her, "No, you don't see. What if we all should become trapped here? Fernando knows we're in Spain."

"—My God—!" it's my own voice I am hearing now.

"Why should I believe you?" she rings with accusation, "With your history!"

"Then don't," he counters. "But I see what I see. His Imperial Highness is my responsibility. We will head back across the border tonight."

She puts her hands up with a tightening of her chest. She has not seen her son since he was four years old. "No—No, wait. You—You're right. This does change things," she agrees. "It's time that Charles takes his rightful place. But whatever we do, Fernando must be informed as soon as possible."

"This can't be allowed to happen!" I'm beyond rational thinking, imagining she can hear me, "Juana!!"

"Very well, we leave at first light," she nods, and Chievres swings open the door.

The Queen is taken aback to discover two more Austrian noblemen and a dozen soldiers, as well as Charles and various man-servants.

Before she can react, Chievres ushers her son into her arms and fetches a pen and paper to draft a hasty contract.

"They're lying—!" I hear my own voice getting louder and louder, until I am on my feet in the middle of the room. But the maddening scene plays on without interruption. Wishful thinking tells me that I could not be led this far for no reason. I must do something!

"—All of you, please,—" the Fleming's voice develops some psychological echo in my mind, "The Queen wishes your presence for—"

I must do something! But what? Maybe the typewriter! Maybe it is coming through the typewriter, the writings! I can control the writings!

"—the witnessing of a contract transferring to her son and heir," he went on, "His Imperial Highness, Prince Charles of Austria, full authority to govern in her name,—"

I leaped back to the typewriter, almost attacking the page:—*don't dont'don't don't dont dopn't don't JuanaJuana don't sign it*!!!!!, all the time repeating over and over "Don't do it! Don't do it! Juana—Don't sign it!"

"—all the regions and territories of Castile," his voice goes on,"

"Don't do it! Don't do it!" Nothing is working. It is as if I don't exist. It will be the end of her, and I can do nothing, nothing to stop it.

The outrush of energy is so depleting that the words become a jumble. I find my forehead creased hard against the typewriter in tears. For a while, limbo.

When I realize that all has gone silent, the images sunken away, I raise up to survey the office. For the first time, the pages loom foreign and aggressive. How could I be driven to such upheaval, where it is all too plain that I am nobody?

My thoughts begin descending to darker more sinister things, tales of invasion, things of disrepute in the daytime of science. The parallel is disturbing. Yet, am I not the invader myself? To them, I am the ghost, the trespasser, the grave-robber of secrets. Then the question is folded back upon itself.

Whatever is happening, it has consumed Thursday, May the 16th. It is already dark outside.

There is one who could answer. Focusing my gaze into the spaces of the room,—over toward the closet,—by the bookshelves,—the door to the other room,—the bulletin board, I cannot see her, but she is there.

"Who are you?" I ask, waiting.

9

The infamous Room Without Light

If the writings were clogged with my own expectations, I could not tell. Though Juana lived on for another half century, her death is not even mentioned in Simon & Schuster's great reference book, the Timetables of History. For the conscious world, her last chapter was closing. Yet, if anything, the Woman in Black continued to grow even stronger. It was that realization, which moved me to suddenly stand and demand again, "Who are you, really?"

"What is is, and done is done" sprang to mind. Nothing else. The encroaching images began again.

It was dawn.

The rain had passed, but the landscape still sprawled beneath its ominous umbra. It was that deceptive light that only touches certain things and leaves the rest in obscurity. Among those shadows I wandered about like a deaf mute, until the vulnerable feeling arose of congested traffic, which began passing through the room where I was standing.

Soldiers carrying things,—I tried to see past them.

"—just like I warned you," a strained voice broke close at hand. "They've fled. All of them."

Chievres. It was Chievres was in the doorway.

"And Charles?" Juana enters from quarters beyond and halts.

"His Imperial Highness has gone to the chapel," Chievres gestures, "To ask God's blessing for our safe journey. A most enviable young man, Your Majesty."

"And Catalina?" she wants to know.

"With her brother," he assures her. "They have much to talk about."

"Bring Philip's coffin up from the monastery. I want it with us," she instructs him then heads back into the rear quarters again.

But immediately as she is out of sight, Chievres brushes a hand at the others, and they vacate the room. Four soldiers take up position outside and close the door. When Juana returns, he is the only one remaining,—Chievres and a trunk of her clothing.

The pressure in my ears swells into plugs, bracing for a trap. And now what is the blood on my keyboard? It must be from hitting my hand against something.

"You can't just go flying out of here looking like this," Chievres advises. "You've been here a long time. Most people don't even know what you look like. Now, especially with the coffin—I'll draw you a bath."

"Don't aggravate me," she warns.

"We can't help it. The word has already spread," he insists. "And they have heard too many bizarre tales. They are probably lining the road right now."

"Then let's not keep them waiting," she smiles.

"Oh, I implore you, Your Majesty, and for all the saints in Heaven, wear anything other than black," he urges.

"I have nothing else," she dismisses it, "Now stop this. You're only delaying us."

"Oh, that's impossible to believe," he opens the trunk and begins searching through her clothing. It strikes me as particularly weird. Juana, too. She stiffens and eyes him in disbelief.

"What is that trunk still doing here, anyway?" she frowns. "I need it..."

Dawn has reflected a silver horizon over the west, and something outside pulls her attention. "You're making this a.." she mutters and slows with the distraction of it.

Chievres continues searching the trunk and talking into the clothes, "—Like that infamous vermilion gown that gave everyone such a heart attack. Whatever happened to it?"

As she pushes one of the panes open, I can also see what she is looking at. A line of carriages and wagons is proceeding across the bridge toward the opposite shoreline. She turns back to Chievres, who is just standing there now, with a reptilian expression that sends a spike of horror through me.

"You said Charles was in the chapel. Those carriages crossing the bridge," her voice goes brittle. "Are they or are they not Charles'? Already leaving?"

"Yes," he drones lowly and unmoving.

She stares at him then looks out again, "—The gates to the city. They're being closed."

"Yes," his atonal response sounds almost unhuman.

"You're leaving me...!" she can barely utter it.

"Yes," he nods, "Only I find these drafts unhealthy. You will need to be moved to more protected quarters, in the interior."

My toes and fingers go numb.

"You—No—Not even you, Chievres,—you would not do this..." she begins trembling uncontrollably, which travels into my own limbs.

"Guards!" he barks.

"There are no quarters on the interior," is it my voice or hers? I no longer can distinguish. "—Store rooms! Those are store rooms!"

"Yes," the Fleming manages an artificial smile, which ends abruptly his control of her.

As he grabs her, Juana goes berserk. The sounds of men at the door set her battling until she wrenches free. Hardly rational, she scrambles into the sill of the open window, teetering there, forty feet above the river.

He grasps her, this time in panic, just as the soldiers burst into the room. "She's trying to kill herself!" he yells. "Grab her! She thinks she can fly! Help me! Grab her!"

Four soldiers grapple with her on the precipice, seizing her arms and legs. But she is more than they anticipate. She bites one of them, while Chievres bounces around out of range, yelling, "Hold onto her! Don't let go! Get her down to the store room! Pick her up! Carry her!"

Hoisted off her feet, Juana collapses into pleading and wailing. Upon this monstrous assault, something inside me snaps. Without fist or form, words or wits, I strike at them again and again, until all is reduced to throbbing.

"Now you see how violent she is and unpredictable," Chievres seems to be saying through my haze. "You can trust nothing. Until she recovers, you will have no conversation, no contact with her at all. The only cure is total solitude and darkness."

For a moment, this throws her into even wilder spasms, as they jostle her out. My heart is louder than the commotion. At the blurry corner of my vision plays-out the anti-episode of Chievres suffering the first real impact of his unconscionable crime, "—What have we done?.. What have we done?"

As I lose sight of him, he is searching for the pouch of Juana's documents, to burn and erase all trace of incriminating evidence, before anyone returns and discovers his loathsome secret.

Suddenly, there is a stairwell, myself being dragged along by the sheer horror of it. Juana is fallen into semi-consciousness shock. Down more stairs we go, darker, turning into a corridor, feeling only the jolt and lurch of their steps.

I remember limbo. I remember my head on the desk. I remember typewriter pages under my face. I remember my hands. I remember closed eyes. I do not remember how long I remained that way.

Yes, I had read of the infamous Room Without Light.

Shame on our species.

Unimaginable,—endless years in a stone cell without window or ventilation, the mother of emperors, kings and queens, it was beyond comprehension.

At 2:55 in the morning I cleaned up the mess on my floor, made new coffee and paced about taunting the silent ghost. I did not want to deceive myself with latent memories. How would I know?

We believe we see a tree in the distance, but we are not looking into the distance at all. We are only interpreting what actually hits the body, whether it be a brick on the head or photons on the retina. We only imagine what must be out there to cause that pattern to happen. At the same time, whatever else enters our consciousness is from another origin, and psychic information follows the same process. That was the dilemma.

Unfortunately, over-think always confounds the spirit, and I had gotten in my own way just at the worst possible time. By now, it was Friday A.M., dark outside. My new beard itched. The village was silent, except for the distant banging of a city truck emptying dumpsters in the alley.

I returned to my desk, still reverberating from those last terrible images. To the monotonous hum of the typewriter, I closed my eyes and irised-down into a featureless deep space.

As the minutes dragged on and on, I resented my wakefulness. But then, what I had taken for a muddy void proved to be a mistake.

It was the Room Without Light.

"At first, I think my face is against the floor, as if I had fallen. But gravity turns like a wheel. I am standing with my nose almost touching a stone wall.

"The vision is internal, for there is no light, just murky surfaces, as a shark perceives the electromagnetic bodies of creatures hidden beneath the sand..."

Where the ears see as eyes, a foot hits against a chamber pot. The numb humming of abject trauma is the only sound that identifies the Queen of Spain, inching her way along the walls to locate the perimeter of her prison. The impenetrable door with its iron lock is hinged inside the jamb. She bumps into a bare wooden table and two chairs on a rug in the middle of the room. She reaches the bed again, with her knees quaking too violently to hold her. Then comes the rustle and squeaking of rats.

"Oh Jesus—!" I raised up to the stinging sunlight of a bright May morning, where Katangi was walking on my papers and soliciting eye-contact. It took a second to realize that there was also someone rapping softly on my door. Jeryll—and Frodo, of course.

She had a quizzical look on her face.

I've been doing some snooping, Paul Casey," she said. She always used both of my names. "Are you aware that the old castle where Juana died was torn down the same year you were born?"

10

How long has this been going on? Are more surprises ahead?—a passage from the book.

—Just what I did not need to hear! For millennia the old castle of curses and ghosts had withstood waves of attack by barbaric hordes from the east. Now, the implication that its dismantling could have sparked something capable of manipulating my entire life was sheer overload. It was the stuff of B movies, Pandora's special effects. Once it escapes the box, you can't put it back. And even if it meant nothing, there was no avoiding the synchronicity. It simply heightened the disturbance of what was going on already.

The next hour of my turmoil may best be said in its translation years later into the novel, JUANA:

◆   ◆   ◆

"The room without light.—Neither day nor night is of this world. Juana has ceased her thrashing and wailing, her screaming and ripping of her fingernails on the thick oaken door. She tries to recall how many times the despised Chievres has shoved food and water inside and left without a word. The three chamber pots are nearly overflowing. She suspects that it may be the tenth day. Maybe.

"She has measured the walls in blackness, fourteen normal steps in one direction, eleven and a half in the other. Bare walls. No sound enters. Not even an air shaft breaks the seams

71

of the stones. But blessedly, a small draft seeps beneath the door, and she sometimes lies breathing it.

"A rug in the center of the room is thick enough to keep her feet warm. Upon it sits a wooden table, but she has moved its two chairs over by the bed to avoid bumping into them. Her garments, in a single trunk, she identifies by feel. Inching about in the dark, she has found no other items, except all of the dishes that Chievres has brought. They are piled in the corner. He takes no chance in trying to retrieve them.

"At the moment, her hunger tells her that he is late, probably by two or three hours. Several times she has fought him in the doorway, only to spill the food,—food that she had eaten later anyway. If she can control herself, perhaps he will lower his guard and at least remove the excrement.

"Suddenly, her sightlessness seems in remission, with a hint of the objects in the room bringing her to full alert. A lantern is sending its glow beneath the door. She moves back and sits at the far side of the room, making no noise.

"There comes the sound of the lock. The door opens slightly. She waits. It opens more, until the silver mirror of the lantern is glaring full in her face. She remains unmoving. Slowly the light lowers until she can see...

11

Denia: the mind-games begin—a better darkness—Norman—the list of names

At first glimpse of his features, Juana tugged the bare shaving of a breath, paralyzed and waiting for him to speak. It was a face I had anticipated from the readings four years ago, the Marquis of Denia. He took his time shining his light about, as if savoring its appalling horror. Even the fluid pace of his movements was chilling.

It was only then, in the light of his lamp, that I realized we were not in the same room as before. The reason was never mentioned, but somewhere along the way, I'm not sure when,—Saturday—they had moved her. At first impression, it had the odor of burned wood. And there was some evidence that fire had scorched the stones of the walls.

The new quarters were somewhat larger, still without windows or light, but cleaner and partitioned into two areas. The main additions to her furnishings were a wardrobe closet and a new carpet of moorish character that spanned most of the floor in the forward space. The bed, which took up a good portion of the innermost chamber, was unmade, and a tapestry stood wrapped about its rod at the corner. Otherwise all was about the same, except that beyond the door there appeared to be some sort of sitting room. I could not tell. It was all too dark.

Denia was fine-featured, about five-ten, with predatory eyes and exuding a confident sexuality. Dressed as if to attend a banquet, he sported stacked heels to make him seem taller and appear more impressive.

When her eyes flitted past him for an instant, the Marquis closed the door and leaned against it with an indecipherable expression. Then reaching into a cloth pouch at his waist, he grew a slow smile and droned, "I thought you might like some candles."

Her devastation played as the silent sting of a wasp. It was my own nightmare that saw it coming, for she could not imagine, but the mind-games were about to begin. And in that malevolent moment the wordless sounds coming with each breath were my footsteps deeper into her darkness.

Comedy relief could not have come at a better time. It was the unscheduled interruption by a tall flashy young man in designer suit, my agent.

Norman expanded through the door in characteristic theatrics, "Where've you been? I gave the signal a million times, and you never picked up. I could have been picked up twenty times, while I was waiting. I set up a meeting with ABC, and you don't even—"

Looking like the test-tube offspring of Tyrone Power and Robert Downey Jr., Norman was a truly wing-ed creature prone to theatrics. But that's another book. He discovered the room after about four steps in and came to a gaping halt, "— Mama mia, gawalt!"

There was no subtle way to begin. As party to the frustrating search for Juana-material in 1970 and his overactive flare for drama, there was no convenient way to inhibit it, either.

"A past life!" he exclaimed, scooping up and scanning the pages, "You have to find out how you died!"

"Norman, you're going to find out how you died—" was all I could get out before—

"I'm telling you," he went on, "I've been transgressed a dozen times,—" He knew the word, but purposely misused it for effect, followed by twenty minutes of et cetera. I was ready to be alone again.

"We should go find out. There's this guy. Let me call him right now," he reached for the phone.

I put my hand on it to stop him, "Okay, this is enough. It's destroying the entire mood."

"All he does is put you trance," he argued.

"I don't want to talk any more right now," I said.

He reached for the phone again. Again I stopped him.

"Watch the wrist," he recoiled. "You were probably Denia, himself—!"

Nothing was ordinary with Norman. Somehow, he could inveigle his way into any production office in town. I have to give him that,—he could sell, from Lassie to Baretta.

"I was Lady Godiva in the Eleventh Century," he chirped. "It's true. I knew all kinds of things that there was no other explanation for."

"Well, if you can't find an explanation, no one can," I agreed. He had told his girlfriend Mary that the reason he wasn't having sex with her any more was that her vagina was crooked.

"We should have a séances," he bubbled on, "Get Tracy to do a number—She knows Peter Hurkos. He even has her read for him."

The third time he reached for the phone, and the third time I stopped him.

"I'm just going to talk to Tracy," he argued.

"Fine," I said, "But do it from your own phone. I don't want to sit here listening to it."

As I opened the door for him, he picked up some of the pages, "I want to take these with me."

"You're going to get transgressed right here, if you don't give me those and take off right now," I said, leading him into the doorway.

"Take off everything (gasp)?" he feigned a Mae West, "Mm-m. Right in the doorway! Well, if you can squeeze me into your schedule—"

"Get out of here," I gave him a push, shut the door, then looked around, "...Katangi? It's safe now."

After the dust cleared, I opened a box of crackers and started back to work.

The sensation begins as if you might sit with your elbows on a table, look down, close your eyes and press your ears shut. The physical world seems to collapse outside in,—right into your head. That's the way the scenes arose again, my fingers chasing after.

Actually, it was not at all as I expected. Denia promised to work for her release, insisting that he had only limited authority. He could only ask for favors,—recommend certain changes. He was in as compromised a position as she. It was, after all, a reasonable assertion.

But that soon filtered into more menacing observations. True, she was moved into new quarters, but only for the convenience of tighter security and isolation. There was only one access in and out of the sitting room beyond, and that opened onto a long corridor lit only by two niche-lanterns. It likewise had a heavy lock on the door.

Juana often rubbed her wrists. Somehow it set the deepening tenor of my writings for the next twenty-four hours.

No one but Denia ever entered the room. His comings and goings were erratic. He always locked the door during his visits, and the guards were stationed well out of sight in the corridor.

Best described as a story told in the bellows of an accordion, the impressions welled and collapsed, often vague, occasionally intense, but always following a central theme. He would build her hopes, joke and flatter her, request her preference in meals, then precipitate some unavoidable obstacle. An emotional roller-coaster, it was classic brain-washing.

In the meantime, another serpent raised its head. I was alarmed and angered. Obsessed with is trophy, Denia betrayed his psychotic libido by probing at his genitals when she was not looking.

Systematically, the rules of proper behavior were breaking down. He would find ways to physically touch her, test her, always in the guise of friendship. For weeks he hatched an elaborate plot, ostensibly with the guards' cooperation, which would smuggle another woman in to temporarily take Juana's place, while they made their escape in a flour wagon. In exchange, Juana would guarantee his pardon for any involvement in the treason. She, of course, agreed, whereupon he acted upon the impulse to kiss her, an offense that exploded in rancor. She wept for hours in pitch blackness after he left and took away the candles. Predictably, she accepted his apology the next day.

Whether in indignation or jealousy, I indulged myself more and more uncontrolled outbursts at his increasing liberties with her. I would get up, pace around reviling him, then go back to the typewriter. It did not matter, behind that bullet-proof glass. In those hours of strangled rage I realized that the Woman in Black was indeed answering my question. It was the hell of her sleepless grave.

Another time, Denia sat transparently cheating at cards and denying it to her face while she watched him continue to do it. It invoked a freaky disorientation, where sensibility had no place to rest. For hours it sucked me deeper and deeper into the mire of confusion.

In 1974, handcuffed to those moments, I could not have identified what was happening to me, myself, but there is a medical reality to it. Only in these last few years, as sole care-giver to a failing parent, have I come to understand the devastation of prolonged stress with no control over its outcome.

It had a parallel, the mercurial volatility of emotion, the vacuous pit of my stomach, the maddening hopelessness of any conclusion. Exaggerated by the flickering candle and shadowy stones, Saturday became the night of its most evil secrets.

With no other thought, I found myself clinging to her, that in some irrational way I might remain a support and companion through the last terrible years of torture. It did not occur to me until long afterward that, in fact, the driving passion might be far more than I would be willing to admit. It never occurred to me. I just did what I did.

Then, to my surprise, it all twisted about. I was unprepared for: "Get up," it began. "Stop groveling like an animal." Denia was entering the room without light in obvious agitation.

"Wherever I sit rests the crown of Spain," came Juana's astonishing reply, "And you enter my chambers only at my invitation."

She was planted on the floor in the middle of the room, and he strolled around to face her.

"I don't have time to waste on your pretenses," he snapped, then made a routine inspection of the rooms to see if anything had changed.

"Oh? And what benefit do you presume to offer the world during that wasted time?" she chided.

He gave a soft snort, "I'm not interested in benefiting the world."

"Then you're an instant success," she delivered in a backhanded put-down.

For a moment, it took my breath. Juana had turned the tables. She had caught onto his tricks. She had learned the game, and by Denia's troubled demeanor, she was playing it better than he.

Under the glow of the burned-down candle, a drying platter of food and goblet of something remained untouched on the table. But it was not until Denia lit a new candle, that I could see her plainly. I was shaken to discover that she was now exactly as the lurid gossip had described her, messy and unkempt. Her hair was uncombed, her face gaunt and without color. She was starving herself.

"My God, I didn't realize how long it's been," I kept thinking, "Has she really gone insane? Certainly, such an endless horror would damage anyone."

Yet, after the initial shock, I began to detect a ritualistic undercurrent so subtle, it took a while to grasp it. The whole ghastly affair had evolved into an elaborate grotesque game,—not cat and mouse, but cat-to-cat.

She had miraculously managed to restore a semblance of social structure, even in the abyss.

"Get up. We've a lot to talk about this morning," he told her.

"Not until I'm properly addressed," she answered.

".. Your Majesty..?" he nodded.

"Yes?" she acknowledged him.

"Get up. Sit on the chair, where I can look at you," he coaxed. "Don't be so sour. You're no fun any more. And eat something. I'm beginning to think you don't like me."

"Well, you're slow, but you show promise," she hummed. "And it's not morning, it's evening. Don't you pay attention to anything?"

Denia erupted in frustration, before he could brace himself. "Who's spoken to you?" he demanded, slinging a chair toward the wall. "Someone has spoken to you! I'll cut his tongue out! I'll castrate him! Who is it?? Who has spoken to you?"

An old scar on his upper lip clefted when he was angry and recast his face with a feral appearance.

Pleased with his response, she gave a cool shrug, "That's right. Throw things. Throw the food away, while you're at it. What a stunted imagination you have, Denia.—Probably from too much fresh air and sunlight.—

If you want to know, it's no mystery. In the morning, your face is puffy and wrinkled from sleep. But in the evening, it's simply coarse with depravity,—which is how it is now, you wicked boy. It's evening. And send someone around to pick up the chair, when you're finished having this infantile tantrum."

Her lightning retort released me into wild paroxysms of jubilance, bouncing in my chair. From the rage on his face, I expected him to strike her. But he did not, and it suddenly occurred to me why. I could see it in his eyes. Juana was Spain,—which by proxy made him emperor, Emperor of the Room Without Light. Its walls had become an alias for logic. Denia was the curse personified. It was he who was mad. A shudder took me.

As it went on, I felt physically in the cross-fire, contaminated. The stale air of her room brought a hurting sensation in the bottom of my lungs, while their bizarre skirmishes continued, one after another after another through the night.

Sometimes sweat would run into my eyes and burn, so that I would squint and tire my whole face. The pages did not keep up with it.

It is about nineteen days into her fast that the Marquis breaks down and extends the olive branch in a rare moment of contrition. He is anguished that circumstances had run amuck with them. But it is too late. They have gone too far. He is as trapped as she. In demonstration of his remorse, he brings gifts to improve her circumstances,—fresh flowers, her silver candelabra, a red satin bedspread, books.

She struggles to her feet and trails behind him in bewilderment as the gifts keep coming, her beloved guitar, golden goblets, a new table and chairs, filling the room with them, until it resembles a royal boudoir. Mesmerized by such lavish and uncharacteristic capriciousness, she takes a long time to speak.

"Are you above taking a bribe?" she ventures, "Certainly it can't lessen my esteem for you."

"A bribe?" he scoffs. "You have nothing, only me. Everything that belongs to you, we have already."

"Oh, it's the other way around," she reminds him. "You have nothing. Only me."

He pauses to study her then strolls about in grave thought. "We would need money,—military forces," he muses, almost to himself.

"We have Cisneros—!" her tones rise in anxiety.

"Cisneros is dead," he says. "Long ago. Anyway, you didn't answer me."

"Answer you what?" she frowns.

Earlier, he had asked if she wanted to visit Philip's coffin. But dismissing it as an empty taunt, she had not answered.

"They say the nuns have a particularly morbid curiosity," he smiles, "that they've even removed certain parts of his trousers to see the bones. Does that amuse you?"

Juana freezes, almost blacking-out. As he turns, she seizes the table knife to end his obnoxious existence. But a shadow warns him, and in a one-sided struggle, he twists it out of her weakened hands.

"He must be a lovely sight by now, don't you imagine?" he gloats.

"If you've finished, I permit you to leave," she calms her voice to answer. "The air is growing foul, and I must conserve as much of it as possible."

He just smiles a terrible smile, "Yes. But I do notice an improvement, since you've stopped eating. The chamber pot has not needed to be emptied so often."

He is aroused by the searing pain that strikes her. "Now, stand up.—Ah, that's very good," he sneers. "And the next time I order you up from the floor, I expect immediate obedience."

She lowers herself to the rug in defiance.

"Juana!" he snaps, "Sit on the floor, where you belong."

Too depleted to continue, she no longer looks at him, "You had better pray that I never again sit where I belong."

She withholds from him the pleasure of her gagging at the savage abuse, until the door has closed and he cannot enjoy it. Then for a moment she hunches, pulling at her hair, before she looks up and stares in disbelief at the surreal color and glitter of the room.

Myself, I can smell the flowers, the jars of oil on the vanity. It dips into suspension, a mirage, waiting for the troll under the bridge. It comes without warning and lethal.

"—Eminence? Your Queen," Denia swings back the door to a ranking Spanish Bishop and another nobleman of the Court. "She won't know you."

Juana's shock is hardly more than that of the men in the doorway. In her rumpled black gown and unkempt hair, she looks certifiably insane.

"..Oh-oh, this is—dreadful!" the pontiff can barely utter.

She rattles out a terrible sound in rising to her feet. But as she reels unsteadily toward them, Denia pulls the men back, "Watch out! She'll claw you!"

"What?" she wails, "He's lying!"

"Please, Your—Don't excite yourself—" the man gasps.

"He's lying! He's lying! I wasn't told you were coming!" she rings too shrill, reaching to stop them.

"Back, quickly! We're bringing on another fit!" Denia warns and slams the door at her outreaching hands.

"Denia, you have contrived this!" she wails. "Wait please, only a moment! I'll be only a moment!"

She stumbles twice in crossing the room to fetch some jewelry, straighten her hair and don a cloak. Then returning immediately to the door, she restrains the impulse to pound and raps gently. Seconds drag by. Perhaps they hadn't heard. She raps a bit louder. She is about to rap a third time, when the door opens.

"Majesty?" Denia smiles in supplication, as if nothing at all had happened.

"I'm ready to receive him now," she says.

He cocks his head with a puzzled frown, "—I beg your pardon?"

"You may show them in," she says.

He hesitates, as if confused, "Oh, yes. I'm sorry, Your Majesty, but I'm afraid it's too late."

"What do you mean it's too late?" she demands.

"They left hours ago," he sighs innocently.

"They walked out this door not more than a moment ago!" her shaken reply echoes, as if recanting itself even before she ends the sentence.

"But they wished me convey their most sincere prayers for your recovery," he genuflects, steps back and closes the door.

The brutality captured in his calculated turn of the lock drains the blood from her face. The Court will believe the bishop. To the rest of the world she is no more. Almost imperceptibly, she leans, buckling and sliding against the door, all the way to her knees before the sounds reach her lips. Then, as if born in the caverns of the earth, they come from everywhere, sobs no normal human could endure.

In my soul I kneel beside her on the floor, petting her hair, her cheeks and begging, "Oh, Jesus—Don't, please—! I can't bear this. You're breaking my heart...!"

Putting my arm around her, I kiss her hand and forehead, "Listen to me. Never mind. I'm here with you. Come on now, you've got to eat. You have to live. Please."

The next I knew, I was indeed on the floor of my office, face-down and trying to pull myself together, "Come on, this is what he wants. Listen to me; listen to me. You mustn't do this. You've got to eat. You have to eat."

I rolled over and sat up, holding my knees for a long time. Thinking how utterly real it felt to hold her in my arms, it brought back the memory of an extraordinary experience, which proved that it is possible for two people to meet and consciously interact in the dream state.

A composer friend stayed over one night to use the piano. Whatever troubles were going on in his life, I didn't ask, but it was something highly emotional. At any rate, I went to bed in the bedroom, while he later went to sleep on the couch by the piano.

Along about the middle of the night, I dreamed that I walked out into the hall, where he was entering from the living room in a rage. He was so frantic that I had to literally grab onto him and hold him still, until he finally calmed down.

I would never have said anything about it, except that the next morning he confided, "I had the weirdest dream. I don't know why I would dream such a weird thing."

We had had the identical dream at the same time. It is an experience one never forgets. And so had my involvement with Juana grown to feel similarly hinged in a common mid-world. It was intoxicating and traumatizing at the same time. Sitting there hugging my knees from the repercussions of her torment, I was aware that I needed to ground myself. It was beginning to feel too crazy.

Still Saturday, almost five in the evening, I tried calling the magic shop.

Johnny Gaughn picked up the phone.

"It's your brother," I could hear him call out, across the whine and growl of power tools hoping for the best.

The sounds subsided, then came the sonorous greeting, "Pintok. Um, pintok."

"Peenuk a-nekway nock-wus," I answered.

"I was afraid of that," brother said.

It was just the note of sensibility I needed. As kids, John and I had a fake-talk language inherited from Mom's generation.

"You got a minute?" I asked.

He was installing the bubble lines in a flying saucer. That sounded right. "What's up?" he said.

We didn't talk long. I just wanted to bounce off somebody sane. "What's the point? Nobody's going to believe this," I complained. "I'm not an historian. They'll say I'm nuts, and what am I going to say? You had to be there?"

"I know someone who'll believe it," he offered helpfully.

"Yeah? Who?" I wanted to know.

"Frink," he laughed. "Didn't I tell you he was drawing up plans for a square flying saucer?"

"Say what?"

"It was the only way he could figure out where to put the mirrors," he stifled a laugh.

Enough said that Frink is a mutation of Frank and not usually used in his presence.

"—Just keep writing it down and see what happens," John advised. "So what? Who cares if anyone believes it? You know it. You said every day something has come into the office to indicate that you should keep going. Right?"

"Well, except today. If it's Saturday," suddenly I wasn't sure. "It is Saturday, isn't it? I'm losing track."

"So, get over it. Just put me in your will," he laughed.

"Go back to your flying saucer," I told him. "I'll call you."

"Pe-ogament a-waytus," he said.

I did feel more grounded, but I wasn't ready to face another siege like the last one. Some fresh air would do me good.

"Out the back way," I thought. "I won't have to clean up."

Teeming with weekend movie-goers, the parking lot was a-chatter, but just across Le Conte lies UCLA, with its stretch of shrubs and greenery. I was just balanced on the curb, ready to dodge across and take a run, when, "Paul Casey?"

It was Jeryll, pointing to Campbell/Tolstad's Bookstore. There, head-high in the front display window was a stack of their newest promotion: James A. Michener's IBERIA. History of Spain.

"When I saw them putting it up, I decided to wander in.— Not to buy it, of course, just to peruse a copy," she purposely stretched the suspense. "And guess what. Those names you've been writing about and never heard of before?"

My tongue just sat there.

"Well, somewhere in the middle, there's a little list of people who were in attendance at Tordesillas while Juana was imprisoned there."

"—Yeah?" I located at least a syllable.

"I just sort of scanned it," she said, "But I remembered a couple from our conversation, and I assumed you might want to check it out for yourself."

"Are you kidding? Of course!" I said, "My gosh, thanks. I'll do it right now."

Instead, she reached into a bag and handed me a copy of the book, "I confess. I broke down."

Sure enough, back at the office, I found that some of the mysterious names where there. But I knew that was not the real significance. It was the fifth day, the fifth sign.

"Right on schedule," I thought. "Okay, Juana, I believe you. Let's get on with it."

12

Philip's ghost—delusions of a madman—the games collapse—the writings come to a horrifying, crashing halt—the 6th SIGN

Though every page felt vitally important at the time, they all pale at the events to come that Saturday night and the following Sunday morning. Those will be branded into my memory for the rest of this lifetime.

It was late, maybe after eleven. It started as a flash of Denia conspicuously fondling a long sharp knife, while he sat smiling and making promiscuous innuendos. Then a few moments later, it was something else—a tapping. I jumped. I thought, my God, I was hearing the ghost in my room, just as Tracy had described her. But it was something else, something entirely outside of human handiwork. It was coming from the equilibrium.

Tap-tap. Tap-tap..Tap! Syncopated and almost lyrical, it rose, metal against stone, with occasional tik! on the heavy oak door in passing. It was Juana, playing her prison like an instrument, with a metal-tipped rod from the wardrobe closet. "Fantastic!" I gasped. "Brilliant!"

Secreted in years of blackness without outside contact, she had tried many means of getting attention. She had even pushed rags under the door with her blood on it. Nothing had worked. But the one thing that could penetrate beyond her walls was the sharp concussion of her tapping. If others in the castle heard it, if only faintly, they could not help but be reminded that she was still there and think of her, talk about her, bear her spirit back out into the living. Apparently, that was high on the list of Denia's concerns. That was my feeling, as the images came forth. Again, as I later transcribed it:

".... In the light of a single candle she is pacing, tapping a metal-tipped rod on the bare floor. The whole cell is again stark and devoid of color, except for the tapestry, which now hangs upon the wall. But I am relieved to see that she has regained her strength. Her hair is combed and pinned, and she looks remarkably well, beautiful, in fact. I think she is now about thirty-eight or thirty-nine."

"You're LATE. Late, late, late!" I hear her muttering. "You were supposed to be here hours ago."

Actually, Denia has just arrived, but she does not seem to hear him. She only notices after he has crossed to face her. "Oh, it's you," she says.

"I brought you something," he tells her, irritated that she pays no attention.

He follows alongside her, "I said, I brought you something."

She just continues pacing and tapping. "You're deafening yourself," he rasps. But then his attention falls distractedly to the visible cleavage of her bosom, and he pulls out a lovely jeweled comb to show her, "For your hair. Take it. Please."

Without missing a beat, Juana extracts two tiny wads of cloth from her ears, plucks the comb from his fingers and continues on.

"I'm glad you like it," he remarks sourly, then hovers along beside her again, "Talk to me. Why are we depriving ourselves? You're too passionate to be wasted like this. You're driving me out of my senses. I can't sleep at night. I think of nothing else. We can't go on like this. Why can't we make the best of it? We both need love and gratification. It's a human necessity."

"I've heard that your wife is human," she raises a brow.

"Stop it. You know nothing about my wife," he scowls.

"Yes I do," she dodges away. "She's unsatisfied."

His directionless response is more telling than words. The Marquis resumes following her, becoming more insistent by the stride. "If we can't change this situation, what's the point of denying ourselves the one pleasure we can share together? We are both getting older." He runs an exploring hand down her back.

She wheels to stop him with a look. "You're getting old," she observes. "We all know what that means. Women don't have the same problem."

Her rebuff is unacceptable and makes him yet more aggressive. "Stop this!" he orders, raising a hand at her. "Or maybe you'd rather be put in restraints."

"Aren't you getting bold, you little rogue—" she wheedles.

Infuriated, Denia slaps away the rod, hurting her hand, and he is immediately chagrined, "All right. All right. You can have your infernal musicians—! Just stop this noise."

"When I hear minstrels playing," she agrees. "In the meantime, you understand that I have no choice but to play my own compositions…"

She gestures toward the fallen rod, and he heads away to fetch it, by way of an apology for hurting her.

That's what it is all about! She has been insisting to hear, not musicians, but minstrels. Brilliant. A huge difference, and he doesn't make the distinction. Their lyrics, of course, are the traditional carriers of current events, the living history of the day. She is after the news!

But something far more consequential is already brewing. It changes the course of everything. In his determination to quiet and seduce her, Denia has been reckless and made a serious mistake. He has left the key in the lock. Juana and I see it at the same time.

As Denia turns to fetch the rod, she darts to escape. But there is no time. She just grabs the key and hides it in her clothing.

"Let me be the husband that God has meant for you!" he pleads urgently, turning back to face her.

Something bloodcurdling in his eyes bespeaks the delusions he has built for himself in the deep space of sanity. But if she knows, her answer still plays the game.

"We can't succumb to this, even if we want to," she sighs, supplying just the right hint of encouragement. "There's no return from it."

Instantly, he effervesces, boyishly extolling the mystical bond that has befallen them, "Don't you understand what's happened here?—Think—! Nothing short of this could have stripped away the barriers that lay between us!"

She flirts with coquettish indecision, while he advances his most extraordinary revelation, "It finally came to me. Don't you see? The entire world has engaged in this destiny! It's God's will. There's no other way it could have happened—for us! Preordained, together in this place!"

She drops an aside, knowing he is no longer processing her words, "Yes. How clever, to perceive it as a gift."

On he goes, "God has lifted us out of the world, above the souls of other men. As surely as we stand here, we are the proof of it—!"

Tenaciously, he attempts to undress her, but she pulls back in modesty to begin undressing herself. It precipitates his uncontrollable excitement, and he starts disrobing himself faster than his trembling hands are able, "Yes-yes, my darling! Yes!—Oh, yes!"

Slipping out of her shoes, she asks him for the courtesy not to watch. He understands. And as soon as his back is turned, she silently swings wide the door. Then only four steps beyond, she opens the door to the corridor, exposing his babbling nakedness to the flabbergasted guard.

My outburst of elation is uncontrollable, with the outrageous spectacle of the struggling Marquis, a patch of scraggly black hair above his bare buttocks parted at a funny angle from the crush of his belt, his voice rambling and fluttering, "Do you think you suffered Philip's infidelities alone? I died to console you. To press myself upon your breasts! To have for myself that private place where Philip—"

Juana beckons the immobilized guard to enter, as Denia realizes that he has over-spoken. It jolts him and he starts to look around, then goes on, "...Oh, yes. I've been keeping track of you. Very well, I confess. I wanted it! To lie in his bed. Where he had been! God forgive me, Juana, you're the only one who understa—"

Discovering the guard, Denia seizes-up like a granny-knot and claps a hand over his privates, too quick and hard, from the looks of his pained reflex. Juana bursts into laughter and the guard snaps to Present Arms.

The appalled Marquis hops to the door and slams it, "You vile—You evil bitch! You've destroyed me—The respect of my men!"

"Oh, be sporting," she tells him. "You hadn't any respect." She hands him his trousers, "Just say you were trying on my clothes."

His veins could be willow branches under the skin, while he jams his clothes back on in a mindless rage, "You venomous snake! You are mad!"

She hands him the key, "Then say it's contagious. That you've spent too much time in this oppressive room."

A major dragon has spread its wings. It is the first time that anyone outside the cell has been privy to the goings on. And to expose him in such a mortifying way, intentionally or not, the Queen has completely reversed their roles. From the looks of the gaping guard, it will be automatic news-flash. The whole castle will know within the hour.

The guard must be silenced. Denia controls himself, cracks the door again and orders, "Remain where you are!"

He finishes dressing, not answering anything Juana says. Then he slaps the candle off onto the floor and steps on it, leaving her alone in the dark.....

Something else should be noted at this point, something which ended up in the writings that night. It epitomizes the saturating propaganda machine that warped everything the world would believe of Juana.

There is record that Juana's keepers had pried a stone from the wall to abduct the young Princess Catalina from under her mother's watchful eye and slip her away to be introduced at Court. But the sheer chronicle of it flags a fraud. Nothing of the claim makes sense. Why would they even mention such a thing in the first place, except to pacify the disgruntled Castilians, who were already suspicious of the secrecy under which their Queen was being held?

Catalina was twelve when introduced to Ignacio, which means that Juana had already been imprisoned in solitary for two years. The girl was old enough to know things and talk. To say that the she was housed with her mother is preposterous. She was out and about in the castle all the time. That is just common sense. There was no reason to abduct her.

It was a necessary lie manufactured years later, to explain what could not be hidden from those in the castle. And its truth unfolded during the beginnings of the sixth day. Sunday.

As often it did, the situation began forming in blackness. At first I felt as if I were lying beside her on the bed. You know how one gets an uncanny feeling? I sensed a third presence in the room. So did she. It was very strong.

Juana stiffened and sat up. There was the stub of a candle within reach, and she struck a flint to light it. In that spark, only a few feet away stood a heart-stopping horror,—the ghost of Philip! Dressed for the coffin, bloodless, with the burial shroud still clinging to his shoulder. He was reaching out at her.

She screamed, as I did myself. In wild panting and paralyzed vocal sounds, she scrambled to beat in terror upon the door. The calamity brought two guards and finally Denia with a lantern.

We looked around. Both rooms. Nothing. She was totally alone. Chattering with fright, she sank her fingers into Denia's arms, not even able to tell them what happened. Probably just as well.

"She's getting worse," he groused, sending the men away and locking her back into darkness.

Suddenly, the blinded crypt was more terrifying than it had ever been before, a cage in the pathway of the dead. She located the candle, shaking so she could barely light it, then sat huddled on the bed with her back to the wall. We waited, while the tiny flame began to dance in an unearthly warning.

".... Out of the murk, the wall at the blackened tapestry in the other room, the ghastly sight again emerges, slowly with outstretched arms..."

"Please, don't hurt me," she stammers. "I know you still lie unburied, but you've had your revenge. Look at me then, what I've become—"

It says nothing. She goes rigid, half-senseless, as its grey hands touch her, then draw her into an embrace. Then, from the outer fringes of her senses, Juana begins to focus more closely upon his face.—It is the heat. It is the heat of his body.

"You realize, of course, that what you're doing is punishable by death," she says lowly.

The young imposter collapses cowering to his knees, "Forgive me! I beg you, Your Majesty! They ordered me! They ordered me to do it! I—...Save me, Madame! Please! Save me!"

So tragic is his sobbing, she lowers a hand onto his head for a long moment. "I cannot save anyone. Go," she tells him.

As he flees behind the tapestry, she follows and discovers that a block has been pried away. A hole in the wall! Her instinct is to escape behind him, but Denia is too quick again at her door to intercede.

She studies her keeper, while he checks the activity outside the hidden escape route.

"Don't waste your time," he says. "They are replacing the stone. You made it easy. Thinking you were so smart. Tapping your silly stick."

"So," she finally inquires, "What doom have you now for this innocent boy? Murder? Because he happens to resemble a prince? What have you planned for him? A boy who obeyed your orders? What reward have you in mind for him? Eh, Denia? And for what?"

He ignores the question.

To his shock, she immediately blows out the candle herself, rendering both of them sightless. His alarm is not amusing, "What are you doing? Don't move! Stay where you are! Did you hear me? Say something!"

Since she makes no sound, he repeats himself in a raised voice, until he reaches the door and sheds light from the sitting room. She has frightened him.

"You should have let well enough alone," she says. "You fooled me the first time. You're a despicable creature, Denia, that you would use love as a weapon. But then, that will be the ghost to visit you in the night.".....

There was no more banter. A new element had entered the picture, a dwindling communication, with Denia's noticeable lapses into depression. My notes became less demanding as their conversations shrank to petty chores. I had more time to think, to interpret what else was influencing the deteriorating changes.

From little hints, the abandonment of the games, the stress and apathy in Denia's demeanor, it was more than personal bitterness. It stemmed from other troubles, troubles brewing on the outside. If that were so, the Great Uprising had begun.

In the microcosm of Juana's cell, there would be no inkling of it, the violence of a grass-roots rebellion sweeping the countryside, bands of guerrilla fighters forming into a people's army, raiding and overrunning the cities,...the shouting of "JUANA."

Over and over, she asked for the chance to communicate directly with Charles. "Don't make me fight with my son," she pleaded, "You already have everything that belongs to me. Let me speak with my son."

She was unaware that the Austrian raft had begun to sink beneath the puppet king on her throne. The people no longer trusted the teenaged heir to Castile and Aragon. They wanted the return of their rightful Queen, insane or not, and time was running out.

This was the new and frightening danger that I sensed in Denia's behavior. This was the firebrand thrust into consciousness on Sunday morning.

I had been typing off and on since about 2 A.M. All the shops of the Village were closed. Though the sun was up, the streets were still empty. Five and a half days had stolen my vitality, when the room without light again began to give notice.

.... Denia sits staring at her across some food on the table. Suddenly, with no discernible forethought, he pulls a dagger out of his belt and says, "Here, drive it through my hand."

Setting his hand palm-up next to the food, he offers it to her, "Go ahead. You always wanted to know how it feels to draw my blood."

She gets up and walks away. He just sits.

Finally, "What can I say?" his deflated rhetoric flows off to the stones, rather than to any real person. The unusual tone of tragedy is beginning to pull at my neck. It is as if something has collapsed and is depleting the whole room.

"Nothing," she says, sitting down on the bed.

He breathes heavily a few times then straightens up, "Oh, I forgot." Forcing a smile, he reaches into a basket under the table and brings up a wine bottle. "Here, I thought maybe a good drink could help get us past this travesty."

He takes her a glass of wine, kisses her on the cheek, then sets the bottle on the table. "Keep it."

She doesn't say anything, and he backs slowly to the door. But he doesn't leave. He just stands there a moment watching her.

Electricity draws my eyes to the wine, as she lifts it up—"POISON!!!!!"

"They did it! They destroyed her!" I slammed myself back away from the typewriter, almost knocking it off the desk, "Oh, my God! Oh, Jesus Christ almighty God!" My breath came in gut-belches. I knew it was poison! I knew it was poison! They destroyed her brain! I lurched up, grabbing my head with a shock too horrible to contemplate. It staggered me almost to insensibility, "Oh God! Oh God!" I dropped to my knees.

".. Juana..!" I just fell on my face on the floor and sobbed there until the ruins of my emotions drained me away into a blessed sleep.

I awoke a zombie. Not a second more of it would I imprint into my life. I ripped and crumpled the mound of pages and crammed them into the wastebasket. It was over.

The sky was clear and beautiful, the sun warm on the roof outside my window. I stripped to my shorts and climbed out to lie there and blank out. Voices and cars in the surrounding Village disclosed the hundreds of people at the bottom of the walls. But no one could see me.

How long was I there? My skin said hours. It was simple overheating that finally drove me indoors, where I once again succumbed to the need for sleep and to escape from the monsters of my anguish. But sometime shortly I was wakened by a banging.

Sunday the building was locked, and the banging came from outside the rear door at the top of the staircase. If it was anyone I knew, they had certainly seen my car, so I couldn't very well pretend not to be there. I pulled on some levis, while the banging increased.

It was Norman, with eyes like baseballs. There was no trace of meaning in his face. I thought at first that there had been a terrible accident. Without a word, he handed me a thin little book.

It took a second, then it came like a punch in the nose. "This is IT??"

Love Possessed Juana, it was the mystery book we had searched for four months and never were able to find. It was not a history book; it was a play. No wonder. Out of print even before Norman was born, it was published by the Twice-A-Year Press in 1939.

"Brandeis Book Auction," he muttered, "Century City." Heading right back down the stairs too spooked to discuss it, he went on mumbling, "Mary is waiting in the car. I'm going straight home to bed!"

I knew something very bizarre had happened, but the whole event was not recounted until days later.

The Brandeis Book Auction, always a huge affair, was spread out under the parking structure of the Century City Mall, where its hundred tables were stacked high with used books of all kinds and sizes.

On the way back to their car after shopping, Norman and Mary decided to take a detour and look at some of the book bargains. They had wandered halfway through the tables before stopping, where he reached down and turned over— this. There was no joking. He bought it for a quarter and came directly to my office.

Nothing will ever approach what was going through my mind, as I stood staring at the summons in my hand, that worn little book,—the SIGN of the Sixth Day.

13

A call to Tracy—work resumes—a tearful goodbye—what Juana needed me to know

I knew what it meant, and I resented it with a fury. Even the suggestion incensed me. Suddenly those words of the stranger four years ago struck home with a vengeance, "You will know things you don't even want to know."

He could not have imagined how right he would be. It was terrible enough without witnessing the details of Juana's premeditated destruction. My beautiful Juana would never be the same. The villainy of her keepers had not died with them. They had broken the spirit that stole my heart and was now banished to a crippled ghost still prowling the cobwebs, defying her long-vanished tormentors. I would not do it. I would not become pall bearer to her disintegration. I refused to brand it into my mind.

I stood there, staring out over the parking lot, where Norman was pulling away, and wondering how I had allowed myself to reach such a state. It was idiotic. Then why could I not divorce myself from some crazy head-trip, whose only earthly evidence lay crumpled and smashed in the wastebasket?

Not until this excruciating moment was I forced to ask myself the mind-boggling question, had I actually fallen in love with her, a figment of my dreams? Had I? Impossible. The bright May sun of the parking lot seemed to say so. It chastised me.

But if it was all so totally crazy, then what does one say to the unaccountable throbbing of his heart? Is that not real? Then, of course, there was the book, the worn little book in my hand.....

All at once something came back so clearly, which I had not thought of in years. It was a bizarre dream that seemed to mean something, but I never figured it out. Nor had I ever mentioned it to anyone. Maybe that was because the time of its meaning had not yet come. Could this be it?

It was a very sexual dream, where that part of me was suddenly dropping into a bottomless black well, faster and faster, farther and deeper, until I knew the connective tissue was stretched so thin it would tear apart, if I did not do something to stop it.

Why did that now come to me so vividly? Was it the foreshadowing allegory that my connection with Juana was in danger of being lost in the bottomless well of time,—if I did not do something about it?

Was there really something more that I needed to see of the awful visions? First I wanted more answers about the haunting ghost of my room. What else could she possibly be about? I decided to return Tracy's call.

Charismatic and voluptuous, to the rest of the world Tracy exuded the image of a prosperous star. In reality, she had sacrificed almost everything she owned to food and vet bills for an army of little stray animals. Her previous apartment manager, in the hills up Gower Gulch, had threatened to have Animal Control destroy all the little creatures she had been caring for for years. So, with only hours to spare, she bought the only place in Hollywood she could afford, a disaster of a crooked little shack south of Sunset.

We picked a dark night under a winter downpour to smuggle the little refugees in, so her new neighbors would never suspect. Rain was pouring in through the light fixtures in the ceiling, and I was on the roof, trying to plug-up the leaks, when I heard her crying in the room below.

I found her sitting on the floor wondering what the hell she had done. With her long red hair bound up in a damp swath of something, she had started to hang a big picture to camouflage the lumpy walls, when the hammer went right through into the next room.—Anyway, the little beasties were saved and alive, and that was where she now answered the phone. I caught her getting ready for work at the club.

"It's about time," she said.

"I know," I apologized. "I'm Sorry. I've been working. I just stopped to follow up on your message."

"Which one?" she asked cynically.

Without going into detail of the last six days, I brought her up to date with the mystery book that Norman had found. Almost instantly, a woman's face came through to her, which Tracy believed was Juana. Ironically, she was describing the exact image of Angna Enters, who had written the play, "Love Possessed Juana." And it was Angna herself, who had performed in the role of Juana.

"But what I really want to know," I went on, "is if there is anything else you can tell me about your impression of the Woman in Black."

"Well, the little I could see of it, her hair looked light,—grey or blonde, maybe. I'm not sure," she recalled.

"I mean, like her state of mind," I became more specific.

"I told you, she's very impatient," Tracy said. "That's what I'm getting. She's a very strong woman, tapping on your desk to hurry-up and finish."

"...Finish?" Knowing what had happened, what else was left? It felt as if the presence around me was just obsessed and could not stop, like a thread unwinding to the end.

Perhaps she was, after all, the final product of all the damage they had done. What was I dealing with? I wanted to know. It mattered.

"Hello. Why do you keep repeating me?" Tracy said, "Come by the Club. I've got to get ready. We'll talk there."

"Okay, maybe," I said, and hung-up unanswered. I looked around for Katangi.

Nothing was the same as before. All had gone negative. My sunburn was beginning to itch. But in the end, it was not the Woman in Black for whom I would finish the journey. It was the woman with whom I had fallen in love, to hold her hand, even if she would never know it.

I took the cover off the typewriter then climbed up on my chair and squatted there, staring at it, as if I were a frog and it were a bomb or something. The expectation of catastrophe bore into my temples like teeth. It was hopeless. She had no way out. She had nothing, except what her keepers brought her.

Sheer survival instinct tried to will it away, as the moments dragged on with nothing happening. I finally settled back down into my chair, leaning only inches from the hammers of the typewriter, and just rocking there. She needed to end her story. How terrible.

A foul odor wafted into my senses and hung about. Then the stones of her prison sprang full-blown with an image that expelled all the air from my lungs.

".... There she sat, her hair hanging loose, picking at her pillow. Picking, picking. "Oh, don't let me see this," my mind recoiled."

It was a replay of the state mental institution, where I had researched a story for Frank McCarthy,—a ward where inmates' hands were bound to keep them from picking their skin bloody.

Denia was gone.

Picking, picking, she kept picking, pulling the feathers out, one by one and dropping them on the bed. "Oh, my God!" I looked around, trying to control my wits, "Wine! Wine, where is the wine?? How much did she drink?"

—There on the table. The bottle and glass. Red wine. I couldn't tell how much she might have drunk. There was some in the glass, but I had no hands to rescue her from it. My eyes were swimming and my chest cramping.

"What have they done to you? What have they done to you?" was all I could get out. "Oh, my God."

No token of my turmoil touched her world. Her world was silent, surrounded by shadows and stone. Picking, picking. "See me, hear me, anything!" was raging through my veins. Nothing. Picking, picking.

I bent to her ear, her cheek, that perhaps she would somehow feel my affection, my being there. I started whispering.

Suddenly she stopped, and I held my breath. It was dizzying, as if for a second we were welded metal. I, too, had stopped, stopped everything.

But it was not my presence that had attracted her. Juana had become fixed upon one little white feather, as if it were fascinating. Like a child playing, she took it over by the candle and carefully straightened it out between her fingers and the table top.

It was agonizing to watch. She meticulously aligned and zipped-up the tiny bracts of each featherlet, off in her own minuscule universe. Then, when she was satisfied or bored with that, she dipped it into the wine, coloring it red.

The fetid odor I had smelled was coming from the crock beside the bed. I began noticing other things. It looked as if Denia had not been there for days. There were several apples, mottled and wrinkled from storage. And some cheese. And water. Had he gone away and left her on her own, with no one to attend her? Apparently.

—And what was she doing now? She was holding the little feather up and looking at the candle flame shining through it. At that instant, the dire sadness of her face was something unearthly. It was all I could do to sit beside her emptiness and whisper unheard things, until the little feather was entirely dried-up and its pretty red gloss shriveled away into wavy crusts of sediment.

She set it down and crossed to lie on the bed. As she pulled her feet up into the fetal position, I thought I heard her begin to cry.

I leaned to kiss her. "I'm here. I'm here," my mind said, "Don't cry. One day, it is you, who will find me again. And all this will be past."

◆   ◆   ◆

That was it. Good-bye. It was over, gone, finished, burned out, the woman in black, everything, all ending at the wrong place, more awful than before. It was just my little office in the Village.

It felt weightless. I didn't want to speak to anyone, not Jeryll, not Norman, not Tracy, not even Katangi. There was nothing to say. I was embarrassed by my own emotions. I didn't want anyone to know. I went for a run. Katangi was waiting when I got back.

It wasn't until the next day that all the niggling little details began to squirm. Surely there is a reason for everything. Something was missing. What? What had it gained, those last assailing images, but to embitter me against the phantom that had wrought them.

Could I have gotten it wrong, embellished it with my own preconceived notions? To push my ego out of the way, I tried to imagine what Dad would be looking for at the same crime scene. What inferences would the detective draw? What notes would he take? It didn't work, quite, but I went back over everything I could remember. There had to be some reason.

Yes, there was the one thing: Denia had been gone and left her alone, apparently for days. What would that mean? I went back to the library books.....

During the final stages of the Great Uprising, the Austrians suddenly found themselves fleeing for their lives. The ship to rescue them was already standing offshore, and the outrageous irony was that the only person in the entire empire who could save them was Juana. As Chievres and others galloped, hat in hand to Tordesillas, barely ahead of the insurgents' Communeros Armies, they must have been wondering how they could confess everything they had lied about for years, and then persuade her to sign a declaration repudiating the very people who were on their way to liberate her.

Remarkably, the records reveal that, even after all they had done to her, even so, she agreed that if the full Council approved it, she would accept their recommendation. Otherwise, she would not sign anything. Of course, there was no time left for her captors. THAT does not sound like the judgment of a brain-damaged person. On the contrary, considering the circumstances, it was about as sensible as it gets.

Additionally, if she were as mad as they claimed, how does one explain her famous address to the Court, following her release from prison?

That, then, became the detective's question. If I was not seeing the simpleminded child's play it appeared to be, then what was Juana doing?

I phoned John,—the magician.

"She dried the feather by a candle?" he asked. I could hear his mind whirring already.

"You could say that," I conceded.

"Do you remember what it looked like?" he asked.

I thought so.

"She was testing for poison," he said.

"You think?" I was stunned. But on second thought, why not? Such things were commonplace in those days. It must have crossed her mind, particularly after Philip's abrupt and inauspicious end.

"Sure. Come on over," John said, "Let's try it!"

We did. That evening we reenacted the exact same procedure, just as she had done it, some with pure red wine, four others containing different things like aspirin, bug spray and silver nitrate.

John was right. Sure enough, three of the four with additives showed little striations of sediment, while the plain wine dried clear.

She knew! Juana knew. That was the thing she needed me to understand. That was the bleak expression on her face. That's when she curled up and cried.

So? Now what?

In the office, things returned to normal, or as normal as they could be after that. I finished my work on the teleplay. But the ghost from the Sixteenth Century apparently had not finished her work. Through the ensuing years, the comment would be heard a thousand times, "Juana is at it again—!"

14

In the mid-seventies, the country was galloping with aggressive youth and rebellion, challenge and change, in answer to the wilted flowers of the sixties. The front line casualties of the Viet Nam war had been playing on prime time, a United States president and a senator had been assassinated, American politics seemed a vacant disillusionment, porn was on the corner news stand. Spoon-fed ideals were keeling over like the redwood forests of the northwest, and the U.S. was rudely awakened to its own Shenanigan Junction, D.C.

If it all seemed familiar, it was. Juana's Hapsburg saga was the perennial high stakes, trampling anyone in their way to glory and the buck. I thought the time was perfect for the American public to relate. I would write the play.

At first, I regarded the mess of pages as a sort of play, anyway, because of all the dialogue. In my mind, it was the unmasking of treason and gaslight on the grandest scale, the Hapsburg takeover of Spain. They stole half the world and got away with it. Most tragic of all, Juana's worst betrayers were the three men she loved most, her father, her husband and her son. It seemed a classic theatrical drama.

But after ten days of sorting it out, there was no structure, just an endless outpouring of grievances. There were shadow-people that could never be crowded onto a stage. It was just a rambling disjointed jumble.

It would be no piece of cake. But it had become personal now. And so, at the farthest edge of her empire, a five-century butterfly in its cocoon had hatched to dry its wings in the California sun. I promised Juana she would have her day.

Its first version was four hours long, trying to keep everything true to the facts. I can still hear Val Bisoglio's mafioso voice rasping at one of the excess characters. "Forget the truth," he said. "She's in the way. Kill her."

The next and shorter version, only three hours long, I entrusted to the critiques of four close friends in the business. Franklin confessed that he only read it because I wrote it, but he walked around for days afterwards with a lump in his throat. On the other end of the scale, Cynthia Sullivan, crackerjack director, summa cum laude from USC Cinema, said she laughed on every page, "That woman has an answer for everything."

In the end, two liked it. Two hated it. It was back to the drawing boards. Out came a new version.

Pamela Hedley was over at Universal. Executive secretary for David Brown, she volunteered to forward a copy of the new manuscript to Glenda Jackson. I was elated. But six weeks later she called, apologizing. The script had never gone out. She had had the letter in the typewriter a dozen times, but every time something unexpected interfered to stop her.

It was the beginning of a new phenomenon. It would become the trademark of the Juana material. It did what it wanted. It wasn't ready.

I could only see it looking back, but the truth was, I wasn't ready, myself. I had written TV, film and musicals, but play writing is a different animal, and I had not developed that skill. That, however, was about to be fixed as well. One night, after performing my musical for about twenty people at

Barbara Poe's place in Mandeville Canyon, I suddenly landed a patron. Arriving late and only hearing the second act, she was heiress to the Bank of Tennessee, Helen Thompson.

"You should be writing for the theater," she said. "Forget the television crap and get used to living on both sides of the pond." With that, she promptly sent me off to Sunningdale, England to write a play.

It was autumn of 1980. There were yellow-and-red leaf storms in the woods, funny little busses, country mansions set back from the road and the grassy fields at Stonehenge. I had Pear Tree Cottage all to myself for four months in Windleshim and returned home with a new comedy, "Full Speed Awry." Only then did I get the sad news that my wonderful landlady, Sarah Lee Wetherby, had died. The bank had taken over the building, and my rent had jumped from $375 to $2400 overnight. It was time to leave the Village.

It was also time for another dance with Juana.

John had come by to help me pack, and I left him shoveling all the loose stuff into bags and boxes to toss in the car, while I dashed across the parking lot to pick up a last printing job from Multi-Copy.

"Hey, Casey," I was stopped by Curt, the assistant manager. "I'm running-off something you might find interesting," he said. "If you want to come back in an hour, I'll make an extra copy for you."

It was the book of the Birth Cards, Sacred Symbols of the Ancients, by Randall and Campbell. Neither John nor I had ever seen it before, and curiosity, of course, made us look to see what our cards were. But since there was no time to stop and read it, John took it home with him when he left.

Not two hours later, I was pulling all the stuff off the bulletin board, when an obstreperous little yellow scratch-paper escaped the bag and fluttered away into the middle of the floor. It was basically trash, and I might have left it for the vacuum. But I didn't. It had been sitting underneath everything else since my first plans for Spain, undisturbed for eleven years. On it was handwritten in pencil: "Juana de Trastamara, Nov. 6, 1479, Toledo."

...Okay....

I called John and without explanation asked him to read what the book said about November the Sixth. This is the abridged: "ACE OF DIAMONDS—The Card of Sorrow. A life of insurmountable obstacles. A war between love and money. Choose the one, you lose the other. Worse for a woman than a man. Early life dominated by a powerful woman, usually the mother. Fear of the poorhouse or becoming a ward of their children.—Love of the theater..."

I listened, just absorbing it in amazement. "Who does that sound like?" I finally asked.

"Nobody," he said.

"It's somebody," I said. "Who can you think of in all of history that fits that description?"

"You're kidding!" he said. "Juana. She's at it again."

"Yeah. Will you look in the back," I asked, "and find out where her card is on the chart."

There was a pause. "You sure you want to hear this?" he asked. "It's touching yours, end-to-end, under Neptune—the Ruler of Dreams."

15

*The Lombard house—Los Angeles Playwrights
Group—the green ghost—Anna*

The next two and a half years I spent in the old Carole
Lombard house at 7953 Hollywood Boulevard. It brought a
swarm of changes, while the play continued doing its own
thing, linking one coincidence after another.

At a strike meeting of the Writers Guild, I sat next to a
playwright who had not even intended to be there. Jim
Inman. At the last minute he decided to attend, missing his
own birthday party. That encounter led to my submission of
Full Speed Awry to the Los Angeles Playwrights Group. Had I
known that it was a scholarship organization so elite that it
never even advertised, I would not have had the nerve to
submit my poor script. But miraculously, six months later, I
got the call.

Congratulations.

How much I needed that training soon came as a jolt. At the
first session, I didn't know what they were talking about.
They might as well have been speaking a foreign language.

How much the play needed it was paraded in the feedback
of its first reading: "You have a foreign subject, an obscure
main character who is a victim with no victory, who is
subjected to relentless dehumanizing torments, who doesn't
do anything in a grim dark room and dies in prison."

—Well, if you say it like that, it was definitely the furnace to smelt-out the ore, if anything could. I braced myself and went immediately back to work on it.

The Lombard place had two baby grand pianos fitted back to back in the sunken living room and hundreds of pictures all over everywhere. Its famous three gables across the front were obscured from the boulevard by an overgrowth of trees and foliage, which gave it a mysterious aura, even before I knew about its curious legend.

The back yard rose steeply up the hill beyond the patio, with narrow steps and trails that led to little surprise places with benches or tables and chairs. There one could repose in privacy, and I sometimes took my work into the seclusion of the garden.

It belonged to Max Showalter, who was off in New York, readying his new musical for Broadway, and his creative touch was evident in every nook of the premises. So, the old historic place was special enough without the occurrence that happened about two months after I moved in.

I had been sleeping in the small upstairs bedroom at the rear, which looked straight out into the tree branches over the patio. Being alone with all the dark rooms and closets, upstairs and downstairs, made the house seem even bigger at night.

I wasn't quite asleep, my face toward the wall, when that self-conscious feeling crept over me that someone was behind me. I rolled over to look.

There, in the doorway, plain as day, stood a luminous green gown, the shape of a woman, but with no one in it,—at least no one visible. It paused, as if checking on me, then turned and vanished out of sight onto the landing.

"That's a ghost!" I told myself and jumped out of bed to follow.

I was there within seconds, but it wasn't on the landing. The door to the big master bedroom was only a few steps away. So I opened it to peer in. Nothing. Just still and dark. I checked the library. The same. But it had been so bright, I was sure I would have seen it, had it gone down the stairs. Nevertheless, I went down to the living room, the dining room, the kitchen, even the empty maid's quarters. Nothing.

Then, maybe a week later, a man called. He had been watching the old movie *Niagra* on TV and wanted to tell Max how much he enjoyed his performance again, how the film held up even after all those years.

"He may not remember my name," the man said, "But I'm the one from P.M. Magazine, who interviewed him about the haunted houses of Hollywood."

"Hm," I thought.

We talked a little more, then I asked what his interest had been in the Lombard house. "Oh, it's famous for people seeing a woman," he informed me.

I moved my work to the table in the big master bedroom, where I could jump up and write in the middle of the night, if the spirit moved me (so to speak). It was in that room where a second similar occurrence happened, this time with a large black dog.

A stimulating environment, to say the least, I understood why Max found it so nurturing to his music.

I turned out version after version of the Juana play, until the other writers were ready to strangle me. But their merciful relief was on its way. A jag of unexpected and eclectic activities came rushing in from all directions to demand my time.

The first was preceded by a dream.

I was walking in a chalk-white tunnel that I knew paralleled a labyrinth of famous caverns just beyond its walls. So, when

I came to a hole, I climbed through to see what everyone always talks about but rarely sees in person.

It was the Great Chamber, more spectacular than I ever imagined. Fountain-like fans of glistening white limestone rose in mountains. Snowy stalactites dangled hundreds of feet from the domed canopy to meet their clone columns whose feet stood in a sea of milk. It was so awesome and enormous, I was sure I would get lost, if I went any further.

I basked another moment in the spectacle, then turned to find that the hole behind me had shrunk, and a little wooden bird stood in the opening with its wings outstretched, as if to say, "You can't go back."

I knew it meant something. I just didn't know what, until two days later. Barbara called. "Paul," she said, "Our dear Anna is in trouble. She's taken a fall and isn't supposed to drive. Do you suppose you would have time to help her get around to all her important meetings?"

She was talking about Anna Bing Arnold, and the meetings were like Occidental Oil. Her name is in stone at the Music Center, Children's Hospital, the County Museum...One gets the picture—the Bing Theater, the Bing Auditorium, the Bing Foundation, etc., etc., etc..

I went to pick her up one day and encountered a mountainous bouquet almost blocking the entrance hall. "My gosh, Anna," I said, "This looks like they cut down the Big Island of Hawaii. Where did this come from?"

"Oh, you know the man," she said. "He's our president."

On the way to the symphony, she turned to me with the news, "You know, my housekeeper is leaving me."

"Really?" I was surprised. "What happened?"

"Well, there's not enough for her to do. She's going to a family where they have children. It will be more interesting," she said. "My friends tell me I pay her too much, anyway. You know, I pay her four million dollars a week."

"I think it's four hundred," I said.

She shrugged, "Well, whatever it is, it's too much."

It was indeed the Great Chamber of the dream, the movers and shakers, the world that everyone talks about but few ever see. I went to black tie functions in the hand-me-down silk tux of a dead person, its moth holes blacked out with marking pen. Just as prophesied, I had entered through a hole in the wall. And I could not go back.

My old green Rambler had been bashed-in by a garbage truck on the driver's side, and I always left it out of sight in Anna's driveway, when we went out. But one day Armand Hammer came to pick us up and happened to see it. He took me aside.

"Paul," he advised confidentially, "You should drive your other car. This one makes you look too eccentric."

What began so casually developed into a treasured friendship over the next couple of years. Anna had begun her career as an actress on Broadway, so she had always retained a love for the theatre. One day I mentioned my struggle with the play. "Let me read it," she said. She read it overnight.

"This play must be done," she said. "You must get busy and finish it. But give the poor woman some happy moments. And give the actress some action. That's what the audience comes to see." She was right, of course.

But before I had time to act on it, two more projects pushed their way in: the so-called "Power Crystal of Atlantis" and the Neiman Marcus cats.

16

*Sea Mills—Solenz—the Spangled Cats—the play
goes on hold*

From earliest childhood, the same elusive image would occasionally pop up in my imagination. It had features, but I never defined what it was until the late sixties. Then it literally came on like a light.

I drew-up a series of design specs then made a model by hand out of optical glass. It was a high intensity light concentrating lens, which took sunlight from a collector and converted it into a projectable power beam.

By the time I came to the Lombard place, the original lens was long since gone. I had continued experimenting with its surfaces until there was nothing left. But the drawings still existed, rolled up in scrolls in the corner of my old storage unit in Van Nuys.

In 1976, I also had given Atlantic Richfield the suggestion of anchoring submersible generators down in the ocean currents. Unlike the wind, the ocean currents run all the time at a force billions of times greater and driven by the rotation of the earth. Lee Remmick and I made a television commercial called the "Sea Mills," which ran for about a year. But the project itself, like so many other things, ended up in the ARCO warehouse, just a face-lift for the oil company.

So at the time of the '84 Olympics, when Hungarian entrepreneur, Charles Dolesch stayed over on business for a week, we got onto the subject of inventions. I was stirred to bring the old lens drawings out of storage and roll them out on the dining room table.

Even after seventeen years, I told myself, "This is really wonderful stuff. Charles is right. I must do something with it."

Now, if it hadn't happened that very same night, I may not have gotten so electrified. But later upstairs in the library, maybe one in the morning, I tuned onto a PBS broadcast. On comes an animated rendering of Edgar Cayce's vision of the lost Power Crystal of Atlantis. There it was, my lens exactly, firing out its vaporizing beam as it caught the sunlight. I sat riveted, with the narrator still extolling its mysteries, knowing that its equations and blueprints lay right on the table in the room below me.

I called it the Solenz. Unfortunately, the U.S. government would soon step in and put a stop to our manufacture of the lenses. But that's yet another story.

In the meantime, referring back to my meeting with Dr. Leakey and trip to Olduvai Gorge, I had been quietly developing a spotted cat, and Katangi was part of the African branch. Protection of endangered animals had always been a passion, but you never get anywhere clonking people over the head with it. So, the idea was sneaky. Slip in the back door with a loving little pet that would remind us of the plight of their look-alike cousins struggling to survive in the wild. It was easy to keep quiet, all according to blueprint and only a few cats at a time.

But the eleventh generation was the magic number, and voila! In 1982 the first full-blooded Spangled Cats appeared, just as predicted. All at once, Neiman Marcus got wind of them.

So secret that even their attorneys knew nothing about it, a handshake deal was made in the old Carole Lombard dining room, and my little cats became the His & Hers Gift of the year" for the Neiman Marcus Christmas Book of 1986. "A leopard for your living room," is how they touted it in the catalogue.

Suddenly they were all over the news, on the Today Show, Good Morning America, Newsweek, Washington post, American Express, the whole blitz.

But bear with it. It is all leading back to Juana.

My final reading of Juana for the playwrights group was one of mixed-emotions. The play still wasn't working, while the need for licensing a kennel and finding more space necessitated a move into the San Fernando Valley, across the street from the Burbank Airport.

17

The Spangled Cats go to war in the jungle

Katangi's granddaughter Sheba, a pumpkin red with black spots, took Best of the Best at the International Cat Show in the Los Angeles Convention Center. Her cousin Lassik, a gold, followed by winning Best of Show at the big summer event in Paris, France, and was the first California Spangled to become Champion.

Temecula, our calendar cover cat, was a snow-leopard color with blue eyes and, although it was eventually cut from the final release, she filmed a scene with Mel Gibson in Lethal Weapon.

It was in the midst of all this cat-business and filing of lens patents, that I got a call in the middle of the night from A.P. Leonards.

People who buy spotted cats almost always have an interest in wildlife, as well. Tony had become one of my cat-family friends through Neiman Marcus, and this night his call from a pay booth on the road to Lake Charles was about just that.

Tony was convinced that he had stumbled upon an illegal canned-hunting operation in Belize, and he asked if I would go down there with him to investigate. He would send me the tickets.

He was right. A walking arsenal named Bader Hassan, who surrounded himself with a pack of pit bull mongrels, was trapping, tranquillizing and storing jaguars and ocelots, to be sold to foreign hunters for ten thousand dollars a whack. He had already killed fifty percent of the jaguar population in the country, including collared animals from the Cockscomb Game Preserve.

The D.E.A. considered him the most dangerous man in the Yucatan, who pretty much killed people he didn't like. But cutting to the chase, after a lengthy two-year ordeal in the courts, a little volunteer voodoo, a deadly spider bite, a massacre in the secret marijuana fields of Lamanai, a downed drug plane in the gulf and other intrigues, Hassan is now kaput.

That's a whole other book.

With all the pandemonium, it had been over three years since I had attended a meeting of the playwrights group, and Juana was about to pull one of her best stunts yet.

18

Return to the play—Juana, right on time—a
strange woman on the phone—the reading at
Stella Adler's—about Neptune

During the time that everything else was so noisy and my writings set aside, Juana had been silent. That was about to change.

Big producers and directors were calling all the time. I was in their personal address books under "C," but not for Casey,—for Cats. Spangleds, stray cats, persians, alley cats, any cats: "What should I do? My cat stopped using the litter box.—My cat is eating the plants.—My cat is coming in heat. I need to find a home for my cat.—My cat, my cat, my cat..."

By now it was '87. The Los Angeles Playwrights Group had moved to the venerable Pasadena Playhouse, which added great theatricality to the birthing of their new works. And after three years absence, my first night back was exciting.

Chuck Workman was into his celebrated series of film-clip shorts that would soon win him an Oscar. Jim Inman was doing one after another episode of *The Young and the Restless.* Everyone seemed to have shot ahead in his career, except for me. Ironically, it was a playwright named Kitty, who asked, "Are we going to hear that big Spanish play again?"

I left the meeting supercharged, ready to leap up at the crack of dawn and finally get back to Juana.

To set the stage, in my whirlwind move to the Valley, things had been left pretty much as they had been plopped on arrival, unmarked and now grey with dust. After all this time, one could only guess at the contents. That's where the old green Rambler finally packed it in, as well, now serving as a closet for the last load from the Lombard place.

Back inside the southwest corner of the warehouse was the thirty-three foot Kenkraft trailer that my folks had donated to the cause. Its power was hooked up, a godsend during inspections, because with the curtains drawn, it looked deceptively tidy.

This was going to be a special day. I could tell. My building faced the east, where the sun was barely peeking over the airport across the street, welcoming me back to my long-suffering profession. Only one minor chore stood in the way. Before I could start on the play, an important letter needed to be answered.

Searching around, I was chagrined to find only one sheet of stationery left that matched the envelopes. And the only reason that was left was because it was creased. But ingenuity to the rescue, I reasoned that if I pressed it flat, I could still run it through the printer. I would not have to go out and buy more.

The ironing board was in the trailer, and while the iron was heating, I looked for some clean paper to lay on top and keep it from scorching. So, avoiding the blanket of dust, I carefully slid a few sheets out from the middle of a stack on the sink.

Had they actually spoken, "Hi, there," I could not have been more exhilarated. They were my notes from the last reading of Juana,—three years earlier. Not even Sherlock Holmes would have found them. Yet there they were in my hand and ready to go.

"Hi, there," I said.

At Anna's suggestion, a whole new first act brought the spice and passion of Juana's love affair with Philip. It changed the tone of everything. Her terrible ordeal in the Room Without light seemed suddenly a fencing match, less morbid. Still, humungus problems remained. One version even introduced the black ghost. But that didn't work either.

"What are we going to do with this play?" the playwrights grumbled. Cut it down to three characters? Nobody seemed to agree. Then one night something totally creepy came out of the blue with an answer.

It was a dinner party at Franklin and Glady's house in the Hollywood Hills, overlooking the entire Los Angeles basin and its sea of lights, when the phone rang. Penned-in on the couch by a bunch of guests at the far end of the living room, Glady waved to me and said, "It's for you," (her droll Aussie way of asking me to answer it).

Standing beside the big Steinway grand, I was suddenly hearing a strange woman's voice, asking in a Spanish accent, "Is Denia there?"

(Good grief!) "No, there's no Denia here," I said, "I think you have the wrong number."

But the caller recited the proper number and asked again, "Are you sure Denia is not there?"

I called across to the guests in the room, asking if anyone named Denia was there or if they knew any Denia. No. Someone said he never even heard the name before. So, I told the woman again I was sorry, she had the wrong number.

Undaunted, she repeated it a third time, "Are you certain that Denia is not there?"

It was not only her repetitive questioning that rode home with me that night, but Glady's comment, "It's for you." However it happened, who knows, but the answer that came blew me away: Denia was not there. Denia was not there in the new first act. He was coming in too late!

This time it clicked.

Under the direction of Riad Galayini, a concert reading at the Stella Adler Main Theatre packed the house and brought it to immediate hush, as Susan Clark, James Morrison and a procession of twenty-eight actors in black appeared in the aisles on their way to the stage, intoning The Office of the Dead.

A young girl's condemnation of institutionalized atrocities and the scandalous affair with her handsome bridegroom seemed as relevant today as they were to the 15th Century. James' brilliant, disturbing and bi-polar portrayal of Juana's tormentor shot squeals across the audience, beguiling and terrible. Denia had arrived at the party.

There was great excitement leaving the theater. I had barely congratulated myself that the hard part was over, when a voice in the lobby caught me up short, "Whatever got you started on such a story?"

That short answer has led me on a goose chase ever since, for what does one say? It takes a book? And even should I write the book one day, I have no idea how or when it all started.

What I do know for certain is that it did. So, what do you do with the evidence? The event itself was life-altering enough but not remotely as significant as the truth to which it testifies. The overriding message needs no embellishing. Life does indeed continue beyond the grave. The story is true. It happened. We were there.

As for Juana personally? I say, she beat them all.

Oh. And in codicil, before finishing this chapter it occurred to me that the business about Neptune still left one little loose end. What about that guy in line for the movie, who stopped me outside my office thirty-four years ago? When was that exactly? Just as a matter of record, I ought to go check out the date. So, I trekked down and looked it up in the Ephemeris.

Neptune went direct in Sagittarius for fourteen years on November 6, 1970,—Juana's birthday. Why is that not a surprise?

The End

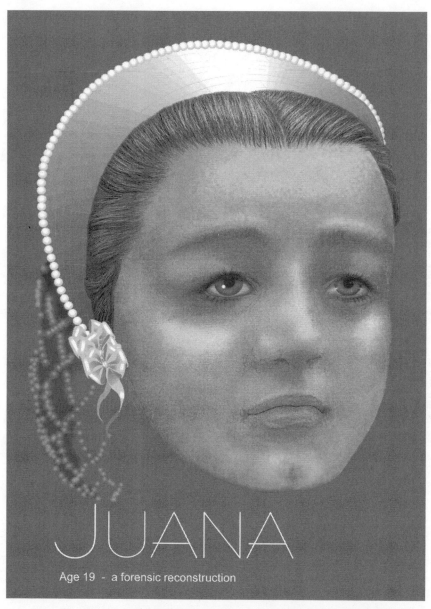

JUANA

Age 19 - a forensic reconstruction

Very few images of Juana exist, and no two look alike. The interesting thing is that the forensic reconstruction looks like the girl in the dream.

EPILOGUE

The hour-glass of life and limbo,
Poured of equal sand,
Sometimes only turns upon
Extending of the hand.

—Paul Casey

In its purest sense, Juana's is not a personal story. It is about all of us. If we are able to operate outside of time and space, even for a moment, it ends the debate. Our identity is not of this physical world.

It speaks to destructive self-interests today even more urgently than to those at Tordesillas five centuries ago, who pursue power and arrogant interests at the expense of the future.

The river of everpresence flows in and out through the transition zone of our dreams, where time and space restraints shut down. There we may open our coffin of human presumptions and be not afraid to explore those wonders beyond this human plane.

As a people, we do not grow where we do not go. Self is the smallest one can be, yet we are all immediate family in the Grand Equilibrium. The joy of life is this never-ending adventure with companions we dare to love.

ABOUT THE AUTHOR

The International Biographical Center of Cambridge England lists Paul Casey among today's top scientists in theoretical physics. His patented beam-producing lenses have been called the lost power crystals of Atlantis. On national television for ARCO he proposed an alternative energy process that runs on the rotation of the earth. He developed the famous California Spangled cats, which were announced by Neiman Marcus. His writings include prime time television, film and stage, with his *Lassie* episodes winning the National Humane Society Award. His photography can be seen on magazine covers and centerfolds, calendars, atlases and posters worldwide. After being Honor Man in the navy, he attended college on a full four-year competitive scholarship. As a child, with only two years of piano lessons he was playing six-year music in recital. To those on the outside world, this is the person known as Paul Casey. But in private there was something else. From the moment he began to talk he startled those around him with prophesies of events to come and recollections of things that happened before he was born. In short, Paul was a psychic. Born December 10th, his birth card is the eight of clubs, a psychic power card.

Kathy Lyon, publisher

978-0-595-35654-6
0-595-35654-0

Made in the USA
San Bernardino, CA
20 November 2012